HIGHER SCORES ON
Math
STANDARDIZED TESTS
GRADE 6

Contents

Introduction

Welcome to *Higher Scores on Math Standardized Tests*, Grade 6. You have selected a book that will help your student develop the skills he or she needs to succeed on the standardized math tests. The items in this workbook have been closely aligned to the Common Core State Standards for Mathematics, which cover grade-level skills for mathematics.

Although testing can be a source of anxiety for students, this book will give your student the preparation and practice that he or she needs to feel better prepared and more confident when taking standardized math tests. Research shows that students who are acquainted with the scoring format of standardized tests score higher on those tests. Students also score higher when they practice and understand the skills and objectives covered on the test.

This book has many features that will help you prepare your student to take the standardized math tests:

- Modeled instruction about how to answer test questions and hints to guide the student toward the correct response
- Test-taking tips
- Practice tests in a standardized test format
- A complete answer key, including references to the specific Common Core State Standards being tested on each question
- A correlation chart of the Common Core State Standards to the questions

If your student expresses anxiety about taking a test or completing these lessons, help him or her understand what causes the stress. Then, talk about ways to eliminate anxiety. Above all, enjoy this time you spend with your student. He or she will feel your support, and test scores will improve as success in test taking is experienced. Help your student maintain a positive attitude about taking a standardized test. Let him or her know that each test provides an opportunity to shine.

Multiple-Choice Items

Multiple-choice items will be familiar to students from other experiences. For multiple-choice items, four answer choices are given. The item itself may be a multi-step problem.

To help students succeed with multiple-choice items:

- Have students solve the problem first.
- Have them find the answer choice that matches their solution.
- Once the correct answer has been identified, demonstrate how to mark the answer.

What if no answer matches?

- Have students restate the problem in their own words to determine the source of the error.
- Then have them evaluate each answer choice to eliminate ones that do not fit the problem.
- Have students work additional multiple-choice practice problems independently.
- Have volunteers demonstrate how they solved multiple-choice problems.

Common Core State Standards for Mathematics Correlation Chart

Standard	Descriptor	Pretest	Lessons	Practice Test A	Practice Test B
Ratios and Proportional Relationships					
	Understand ratio concepts and use ratio reasoning to solve problems.				
6.RP.1	Understand the concept of a ratio and use ratio language to describe a ratio relationship between two quantities. *For example, "The ratio of wings to beaks in the bird house at the zoo was 2:1, because for every 2 wings there was 1 beak." "For every vote candidate A received, candidate C received nearly three votes."*	1	1, 2, 3, 4, 26, 27, 28, 29, 30, 31	2	2
6.RP.2	Understand the concept of a unit rate a/b associated with a ratio a:b with b ≠ 0, and use rate language in the context of a ratio relationship. *For example, "This recipe has a ratio of 3 cups of flour to 4 cups of sugar, so there is $\frac{3}{4}$ cup of flour for each cup of sugar." "We paid $75.00 for 15 hamburgers, which is a rate of $5.00 per hamburger."*	2	5, 6, 7, 8, 32, 33, 34	13	9, 43
6.RP.3	Use ratio and rate reasoning to solve real-world and mathematical problems, e.g., by reasoning about tables of equivalent ratios, tape diagrams, double number line diagrams, or equations.				
6.RP.3.a	Make tables of equivalent ratios relating quantities with whole-number measurements, find missing values in the tables, and plot the pairs of values on the coordinate plane. Use tables to compare ratios.	3	9, 10, 11, 12, 13, 35, 36, 37, 38, 39, 40, 41, 42	9	19
6.RP.3.b	Solve unit rate problems including those involving unit pricing and constant speed. *For example, if it took 7 hours to mow 4 lawns, then at that rate, how many lawns could be mowed in 35 hours? At what rate were lawns being mowed?*	4	14, 15, 16, 17, 43, 44, 45	22, 48	22
6.RP.3.c	Find a percent of a quantity as a rate per 100 (e.g., 30% of a quantity means $\frac{30}{100}$ times the quantity); solve problems involving finding the whole, given a part and the percent.	5	18, 19, 20, 21, 46, 47, 48, 49, 50, 51, 52, 53, 54, 55	29	33
6.RP.3.d	Use ratio reasoning to convert measurement units; manipulate and transform units appropriately when multiplying or dividing quantities.	6	22, 23, 24, 25, 56, 57, 58, 59, 60	20	38

Standard	Descriptor	Pretest	Lessons	Practice Test A	Practice Test B
	The Number System				
	Apply and extend previous understandings of multiplication and division to divide fractions by fractions.				
6.NS.1	Interpret and compute quotients of fractions, and solve word problems involving division of fractions by fractions, e.g., by using visual fraction models and equations to represent the problem. *For example, create a story context for $(\frac{2}{3}) \div (\frac{3}{4})$ and use a visual fraction model to show the quotient; use the relationship between multiplication and division to explain that $(\frac{2}{3}) \div (\frac{3}{4}) = \frac{8}{9}$ because $\frac{3}{4}$ of $\frac{8}{9}$ is $\frac{2}{3}$. (In general, $(\frac{a}{b}) \div (\frac{c}{d}) = \frac{ad}{bc}$.) How much chocolate will each person get if 3 people share $\frac{1}{2}$ lb of chocolate equally? How many $\frac{3}{4}$-cup servings are in $\frac{2}{3}$ of a cup of yogurt? How wide is a rectangular strip of land with length $\frac{3}{4}$ mi and area $\frac{1}{2}$ square mi?*	7	1, 2, 26, 27, 28, 29, 30	10	8
	Compute fluently with multi-digit numbers and find common factors and multiples.				
6.NS.2	Fluently divide multi-digit numbers using the standard algorithm.	8	3, 4, 31, 32, 33, 34	23, 46	20
6.NS.3	Fluently add, subtract, multiply, and divide multi-digit decimals using the standard algorithm for each operation.	9	5, 6, 7, 8, 35, 36, 37, 38, 39, 40	30	3, 48
6.NS.4	Find the greatest common factor of two whole numbers less than or equal to 100 and the least common multiple of two whole numbers less than or equal to 12. Use the distributive property to express a sum of two whole numbers 1–100 with a common factor as a multiple of a sum of two whole numbers with no common factor. *For example, express 36 + 8 as 4 (9 + 2).*	10	9, 10, 11, 41, 42, 43, 44, 45	43	23
	Apply and extend previous understandings of numbers to the system of rational numbers.				
6.NS.5	Understand that positive and negative numbers are used together to describe quantities having opposite directions or values (e.g., temperature above/below zero, elevation above/below sea level, credits/debits, positive/negative electric charge); use positive and negative numbers to represent quantities in real-world contexts, explaining the meaning of 0 in each situation.	11	12, 46, 47, 48	37	32
6.NS.6	Understand a rational number as a point on the number line. Extend number line diagrams and coordinate axes familiar from previous grades to represent points on the line and in the plane with negative number coordinates.				

Standard	Descriptor	Pretest	Lessons	Practice Test A	Practice Test B
6.NS.6.a	Recognize opposite signs of numbers as indicating locations on opposite sides of 0 on the number line; recognize that the opposite of the opposite of a number is the number itself, e.g., $-(-3) = 3$, and that 0 is its own opposite.	12	13, 14, 49, 50, 51	12	30
6.NS.6.b	Understand signs of numbers in ordered pairs as indicating locations in quadrants of the coordinate plane; recognize that when two ordered pairs differ only by signs, the locations of the points are related by reflections across one or both axes.	13	15, 16, 52, 53, 54	32	37
6.NS.6.c	Find and position integers and other rational numbers on a horizontal or vertical number line diagram; find and position pairs of integers and other rational numbers on a coordinate plane.	14	17, 18, 19, 20, 55, 56, 57	8	40
6.NS.7	Understand ordering and absolute value of rational numbers.				
6.NS.7.a	Interpret statements of inequality as statements about the relative position of two numbers on a number line diagram. *For example, interpret $-3 > -7$ as a statement that -3 is located to the right of -7 on a number line oriented from left to right.*	15	21, 58, 59, 60	3	11
6.NS.7.b	Write, interpret, and explain statements of order for rational numbers in real-world contexts. *For example, write $-3°C > -7°C$ to express the fact that $-3°C$ is warmer than $-7°C$.*	16	22, 61, 62	36	28
6.NS.7.c	Understand the absolute value of a rational number as its distance from 0 on the number line; interpret absolute value as magnitude for a positive or negative quantity in a real-world situation. *For example, for an account balance of -30 dollars, write $|-30| = 30$ to describe the size of the debt in dollars.*	17	23, 63, 64, 65	41	42
6.NS.7.d	Distinguish comparisons of absolute value from statements about order. *For example, recognize that an account balance less than -30 dollars represents a debt greater than 30 dollars.*	18	24, 66, 67, 68	28	44
6.NS.8	Solve real-world and mathematical problems by graphing points in all four quadrants of the coordinate plane. Include use of coordinates and absolute value to find distances between points with the same first coordinate or the same second coordinate.	19	25, 69, 70, 71, 72	39	18
	Expressions and Equations				
	Apply and extend previous understandings of arithmetic to algebraic expressions.				
6.EE.1	Write and evaluate numerical expressions involving whole-number exponents.	20	1, 2, 26, 27, 28, 29, 30	24, 47	21

Standard	Descriptor	Pretest	Lessons	Practice Test A	Practice Test B
6.EE.2	Write, read, and evaluate expressions in which letters stand for numbers.				
6.EE.2.a	Write expressions that record operations with numbers and with letters standing for numbers. *For example, express the calculation "Subtract y from 5" as 5 − y.*	21	3, 4, 31, 32, 33, 34	19	17
6.EE.2.b	Identify parts of an expression using mathematical terms (sum, term, product, factor, quotient, coefficient); view one or more parts of an expression as a single entity. *For example, describe the expression 2 (8 + 7) as a product of two factors; view (8 + 7) as both a single entity and a sum of two terms.*	22	5, 6, 35, 36, 37	33	36
6.EE.2.c	Evaluate expressions at specific values of their variables. Include expressions that arise from formulas used in real-world problems. Perform arithmetic operations, including those involving whole-number exponents, in the conventional order when there are no parentheses to specify a particular order (Order of Operations). *For example, use the formulas $V = s^3$ and $A = 6s^2$ to find the volume and surface area of a cube with sides of length s $= \frac{1}{2}$.*	23	7, 8, 38, 39, 40, 41	7	39
6.EE.3	Apply the properties of operations to generate equivalent expressions. *For example, apply the distributive property to the expression 3(2 + x) to produce the equivalent expression 6 + 3x; apply the distributive property to the expression 24x + 18y to produce the equivalent expression 6(4x + 3y); apply properties of operations to y + y + y to produce the equivalent expression 3y.*	24	9, 10, 42, 43, 44, 45	1	24, 45
6.EE.4	Identify when two expressions are equivalent (i.e., when the two expressions name the same number regardless of which value is substituted into them). *For example, the expressions y + y + y and 3y are equivalent because they name the same number regardless of which number y stands for.*	25	11, 12, 46, 47, 48, 49	11	31
	Reason about and solve one-variable equations and inequalities.				
6.EE.5	Understand solving an equation or inequality as a process of answering a question: which values from a specified set, if any, make the equation or inequality true? Use substitution to determine whether a given number in a specified set makes an equation or inequality true.	26	13, 14, 15, 50, 51, 52, 53	21	7
6.EE.6	Use variables to represent numbers and write expressions when solving a real-world or mathematical problem; understand that a variable can represent an unknown number, or, depending on the purpose at hand, any number in a specified set.	27	16, 17, 18, 54, 55, 56, 57	27	4, 50

Correlation Chart
Higher Scores on Math, Grade 6

Standard	Descriptor	Pretest	Lessons	Practice Test A	Practice Test B
6.EE.7	Solve real-world and mathematical problems by writing and solving equations of the form $x + p = q$ and $px = q$ for cases in which p, q and x are all nonnegative rational numbers.	28	19, 20, 21, 58, 59, 60, 61	31	10
6.EE.8	Write an inequality of the form $x > c$ or $x < c$ to represent a constraint or condition in a real-world or mathematical problem. Recognize that inequalities of the form $x > c$ or $x < c$ have infinitely many solutions; represent solutions of such inequalities on number line diagrams.	29	22, 23, 62, 63, 64, 65	14	27
	Represent and analyze quantitative relationships between dependent and independent variables.				
6.EE.9	Use variables to represent two quantities in a real-world problem that change in relationship to one another; write an equation to express one quantity, thought of as the dependent variable, in terms of the other quantity, thought of as the independent variable. Analyze the relationship between the dependent and independent variables using graphs and tables, and relate these to the equation. *For example, in a problem involving motion at constant speed, list and graph ordered pairs of distances and times, and write the equation $d = 65t$ to represent the relationship between distance and time.*	30	24, 25, 66, 67, 68, 69, 70	18	14
	Geometry				
	Solve real-world and mathematical problems involving area, surface area, and volume.				
6.G.1	Find the area of right triangles, other triangles, special quadrilaterals, and polygons by composing into rectangles or decomposing into triangles and other shapes; apply these techniques in the context of solving real-world and mathematical problems.	31, 32, 33, 34, 35	1, 2, 3, 4, 5, 6, 7, 8, 26, 27, 28, 29, 30, 31, 32, 33, 34, 35, 36, 37, 38, 39, 40	4, 49	5, 46
6.G.2	Find the volume of a right rectangular prism with fractional edge lengths by packing it with unit cubes of the appropriate unit fraction edge lengths, and show that the volume is the same as would be found by multiplying the edge lengths of the prism. Apply the formulas $V = lwh$ and $V = bh$ to find volumes of right rectangular prisms with fractional edge lengths in the context of solving real-world and mathematical problems.	36, 37	9, 10, 11, 12, 41, 42, 43, 44, 45, 46, 47, 48	15	12, 35
6.G.3	Draw polygons in the coordinate plane given coordinates for the vertices; use coordinates to find the length of a side joining points with the same first coordinate or the same second coordinate. Apply these techniques in the context of solving real-world and mathematical problems.	38, 39	13, 14, 15, 16, 17, 18, 49, 50, 51, 52, 53, 54, 55, 56, 57, 58, 59	26, 40, 45	15

Standard	Descriptor	Pretest	Lessons	Practice Test A	Practice Test B
6.G.4	Represent three-dimensional figures using nets made up of rectangles and triangles, and use the nets to find the surface area of these figures. Apply these techniques in the context of solving real-world and mathematical problems.	40, 41	19, 20, 21, 22, 23, 24, 25, 60, 61, 62, 63, 64, 65, 66, 67, 68	17, 34	25, 49
Statistics and Probability					
Develop understanding of statistical variability.					
6.SP.1	Recognize a statistical question as one that anticipates variability in the data related to the question and accounts for it in the answers. *For example, "How old am I?" is not a statistical question, but "How old are the students in my school?" is a statistical question because one anticipates variability in students' ages.*	42	1, 2, 3, 26, 27, 28, 29	5	13
6.SP.2	Understand that a set of data collected to answer a statistical question has a distribution which can be described by its center, spread, and overall shape.	43	4, 5, 6, 30, 31, 32, 33	16	6, 47
6.SP.3	Recognize that a measure of center for a numerical data set summarizes all of its values with a single number, while a measure of variation describes how its values vary with a single number.	44	7, 8, 9, 34, 35	25	16
Summarize and describe distributions.					
6.SP.4	Display numerical data in plots on a number line, including dot plots, histograms, and box plots.	45	10, 11, 12, 36, 37, 38, 39	35	29
6.SP.5	Summarize numerical data sets in relation to their context, such as by:				
6.SP.5.a	Reporting the number of observations.	46	13, 14, 15, 40, 41, 42	38	1
6.SP.5.b	Describing the nature of the attribute under investigation, including how it was measured and its units of measurement.	47	16, 43, 44, 45	42, 50	26
6.SP.5.c	Giving quantitative measures of center (median and/or mean) and variability (interquartile range and/or mean absolute deviation), as well as describing any overall pattern and any striking deviations from the overall pattern with reference to the context in which the data were gathered.	48, 49	17, 18, 19, 20, 21, 22, 46, 47, 48	44	34
6.SP.5.d	Relating the choice of measures of center and variability to the shape of the data distribution and the context in which the data were gathered.	50	23, 24, 25, 49, 50	6	41

Correlation Chart
Higher Scores on Math, Grade 6

Name _____   Date _____

DIRECTIONS: Read each question and choose the best answer. Use the answer sheet provided at the end of the workbook to record your answers. If the correct answer is not available, mark the letter for "Not Here."

1. In every music classroom, there are 2 pianos. How many pianos are in 4 classrooms?

   A 2 pianos

   B 4 pianos

   C 6 pianos

   D 8 pianos

2. Isabel compared the cost of popcorn at 4 vendors at the fair.

Snackland	33 ounces for $5.50
Popcorn and More	27 ounces for $5.25
Popcorn King	28 ounces for $5.00
Good Treats	32 ounces for $4.75

   Which vendor charges the most per ounce?

   F Popcorn King

   G Good Treats

   H Popcorn and More

   J Snackland

3. The graph shows the amount of money Paula earns from her babysitting job.

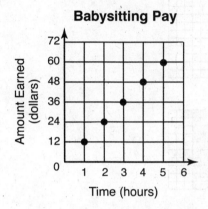

   How much does Paula earn for $5\frac{1}{2}$ hours of babysitting?

   A $24.00

   B $54.00

   C $66.00

   D $72.00

4. The trail around the lake is 7 kilometers long. It takes Manuel 35 minutes to run the trail. What is his unit rate?

   F 2 kilometers per minute

   G 0.2 kilometers per minute

   H 0.02 kilometers per minute

   J 0.002 kilometers per minute

5. Which model has 71% shaded?

A

B

C

D

6. The table shows data from an exercise program.

Activity	Target Rate (kilometers per hour)	Start Time	End Time
Walking	3.5	9:30 A.M.	11:00 A.M.
Jogging	8.5	8:15 A.M.	9:30 A.M.
Biking	19.5	10:50 A.M.	1:05 P.M.

If Tori bikes at the target rate, how far will she travel?

F 5.25 kilometers

G 10.625 kilometers

H 43.875 kilometers

J Not Here

7. Amod estimates that it takes him $\frac{4}{5}$ hour to mow a yard. Which is the best estimate of the number of yards he can mow in $6\frac{1}{4}$ hours?

A 12 yards

B 10 yards

C 8 yards

D 6 yards

8. A total of 2,921 people attended 23 performances of a band concert. The same number of tickets were sold for each performance. How many tickets were sold for each performance?

F 127 tickets

H 129 tickets

G 130 tickets

J 133 tickets

9. Shawna collected 124.104 liters of rainwater during the past 8 weeks. What is the average amount of water collected each week?

A 1.5513 liters

B 15.513 liters

C 155.13 liters

D 1,551.3 liters

10. The combination for the lock on Manual's bicycle is based on the prime factorization of 315. What is the prime factorization of 315?

F $2 \times 3 \times 3 \times 5 \times 7$

G $3 \times 3 \times 5 \times 7$

H $3 \times 7 \times 5$

J $5 \times 7 \times 9$

11. Which situation could be represented by the integer $^+4$?

A A lake is 4 feet higher than usual.

B A $4.00 withdrawal is made from a bank account.

C A football team loses 4 yards on a play.

D A city is 4 feet below sea level.

12. A freezer is set at $-12.2°F$. Between which two integers does this temperature lie?

F -13 and -14

G -12 and -13

H -11 and -12

J Not Here

13. The city park is represented by the point $(-3, 4)$ on a coordinate plane. In which quadrant does the point lie?

A Quadrant I

B Quadrant II

C Quadrant III

D Quadrant IV

14. The distance from Maria's house to the library is 2.35 miles. What is this distance as a mixed number?

F $2\frac{1}{4}$ miles

G $2\frac{7}{20}$ miles

H $2\frac{2}{5}$ miles

J $2\frac{3}{5}$ miles

15. The table shows the average surface temperature of the planets in the solar system.

Average Surface Temperature of the Planets	
Planet	**Temperature (°C)**
Earth	15
Jupiter	-110
Mars	-65
Mercury	167
Neptune	-200
Saturn	-140
Uranus	-195
Venus	464

Which list shows the planets Jupiter, Venus, Mars, and Earth written in order from greatest to least average surface temperature?

A Venus, Mars, Earth, Jupiter

B Jupiter, Mars, Earth, Venus

C Earth, Venus, Mars, Jupiter

D Venus, Earth, Mars, Jupiter

16. Nate recorded the following temperatures.

$-9, -2, 6, -14$

Which list shows the numbers in order from coldest to warmest?

F $-14, -9, -2, 6$

G $-14, -9, 6, -2$

H $6, -2, -9, -14$

J $-2, 6, -9, -14$

17. Which of the following has a value that is less than 0?

  A $|-11|$

  B -11

  C $|11|$

  D 11

18. Last year, Nathan's cat had a change in weight of -12 ounces. Which does NOT show a greater change in weight?

  F loss of 17 ounces

  G loss of 15 ounces

  H gain of 13 ounces

  J gain of 11 ounces

19. Each unit on the coordinate plane represents 1 mile. How far is the grocery store from the dry cleaners?

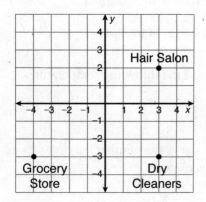

  A 4 miles

  B 5 miles

  C 6 miles

  D 7 miles

20. Gina represented 729 with a base and an exponent. Which of the following is NOT possible? (Hint: Find the prime factorization.)

  F The base and the exponent are multiples of 3.

  G The base and the exponent are equal.

  H The base is less than the exponent.

  J The base is an odd number and the exponent is an even number.

21. There are 16 cups in 1 gallon. Which expression gives the number of cups in g gallons?

  A $16 + g$

  B $16 - g$

  C $16g$

  D $g \div 16$

22. The baker at Upper Crust Pies baked 7 peach pies and 8 apple pies yesterday. She cut each peach pie into 6 slices and each apple pie into 8 slices. At the end of the day, there were 5 slices of pie left unsold. The expression $(7 \times 6) + (8 \times 8) - 5$ gives the number of slices that were sold. Which describes a part in this expression?

  F the sum of 7 and 6

  G the sum of 6 and 8

  H the difference of 8 and 5

  J the product of 8 and 8

23. The expression $\$15.00 \times (n + 1.50)$ gives the total cost for purchasing n number of concert tickets. What is the total cost for purchasing 17 concert tickets?

A $\$232.50$

B $\$256.50$

C $\$277.50$

D $\$382.50$

24. A lock costs $\$15.00$, and an extra key costs $\$5.00$. The delivery fee is $\$5.00$ per order. The expression $15n + 5n + 5$ gives the cost, in dollars, of buying locks with an extra key for n people. Which is another way to write this expression?

F $25n$

G $25n^2$

H $20n + 5$

J $20n^2 + 5$

25. Nolan has 6 boxes of pencils. Each box contains p pencils. He uses 18 pencils. Which expression gives the number of pencils he has left?

A $3(p - 6)$

B $3(6 - p)$

C $6(p - 3)$

D $6(3 - p)$

26. Sheila scored 93 points on her math quiz. She scored 2 more points than Frederick. The equation $p + 2 = 93$ gives the number of points p that Frederick scored on his quiz. How many points did Frederick score on his quiz?

F 85 points

G 87 points

H 89 points

J 91 points

27. Herman needs 4 cups of water to make a pitcher of lemonade. The expression $4l$ gives the number of cups of water needed to make l full pitchers of lemonade. Which best describes the value of the variable l?

A any integer

B any positive number

C a single unknown number

D any positive whole number

28. Dave spent $\$5.00$ on lunch. He purchased a salad and a drink. The drink was $\$2.00$. The equation $s + 2 = 5$ can be used to find the cost s of the salad. Which model shows the equation?

F ▭▭▭ = ▭▭▭▭▭

G ▭▭▭▭▭▭ = ▭▭

H ▭ = ▭▭▭▭▭

J ▭ = ▭▭

29. The graph shows d, the possible number of large dogs that can attend day camp at the Loving Paws Dog Care.

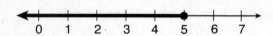

A $d > 5$

B $d < 5$

C $d \geq 5$

D $d \leq 5$

30. The table shows n, the number of people seated in each section of the theater depending on p, the total number of people in the theater.

Total Number of People, p	9	18	27	36
People in Each Section, n	3	6	9	12

Which equation could be used to find n, the number of people that are seated in each section of the theater?

F $n = p - 12$

G $n = p - 6$

H $n = \dfrac{p}{3}$

J $n = 3p$

31. Find the area of the figure.

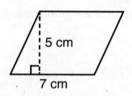

A 12 cm²

B 17.5 cm²

C 35 cm²

D 70 cm²

32. Find the area of the triangle.

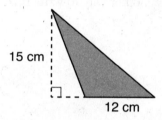

F 27 cm²

G 56.25 cm²

H 90 cm²

J 112.5 cm²

33. Find the area of the shaded part of the figure.

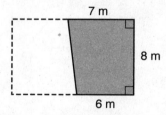

A 21 m²

B 24 m²

C 48 m²

D 52 m²

34. Some of the tiles on Zena's front porch are shaped like a hexagon. Find the area of one tile.

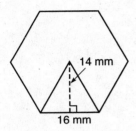

F 180 mm²

G 224 mm²

H 672 mm²

J 896 mm²

35. Find the area of the composite figure by decomposing it into a rectangle and a right triangle.

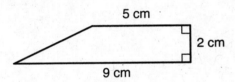

A 7 cm²

B 14 cm²

C 18 cm²

D 40 cm²

36. Trayvon finds the volume of a rectangular prism that is 4 units long, 4 units wide, and 2 units high by filling it with $\frac{1}{2}$-unit cubes.

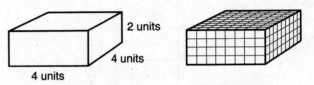

He removes the cubes and counts them. There are 256 half-unit cubes. What is the volume of the rectangular prism in cubic units? (Hint: It takes 8 half-unit cubes to make one 1 unit cube.)

F 32 cubic units

G 64 cubic units

H 128 cubic units

J 256 cubic units

37. What is the volume of the rectangular prism?

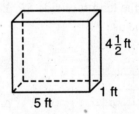

A $10\frac{1}{2}$ ft³

B $20\frac{1}{2}$ ft³

C $22\frac{1}{2}$ ft³

D $25\frac{1}{2}$ ft³

38. Tanya is drawing a template for a parallelogram she will use in an art project. Where should she place the fourth point?

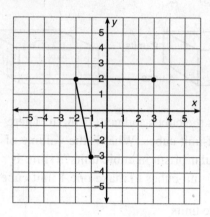

F $(4, -3)$

G $(4, 3)$

H $(-4, -3)$

J $(-4, 3)$

39. David needs to find the length of side *SP*. Which coordinates should he use?

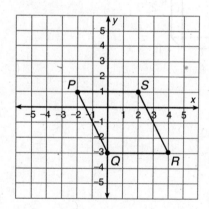

A $(0, -3)$ and $(4, -3)$

B $(2, 1)$ and $(-2, 1)$

C $(-2, 1)$ and $(0, -3)$

D $(2, 1)$ and $(4, -3)$

40. Which net can be folded to form the solid figure shown?

F

G

H

J

41. Cecilia made a net of this rectangular prism. She used the net to find the surface area of the prism.

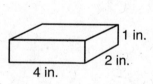 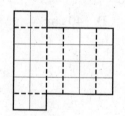

1 in.

2 in.

4 in.

What is the surface area of the prism?

A 8 square inches

B 14 square inches

C 16 square inches

D 28 square inches

42. Students at Kyle's school participate in a canned food drive for one month. The number of cans that are collected each day as well as the number of students who participated each day is recorded. Which is NOT a statistical question for the situation?

   F On what day did the food drive begin?

   G What is the least number of cans collected per day?

   H What is the average number of students who participated each day?

   J What is the greatest number of cans collected per day?

43. Mr. Norris used a dot plot to display the number of questions that each student answered correctly on the reading quiz.

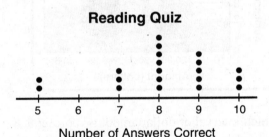

Reading Quiz

Number of Answers Correct

Which statement correctly describes the data?

   A There is a cluster from 5 to 7.

   B The median of the data is 7.5.

   C There is a gap at 6.

   D The mode of the data is 9.

44. The table shows the number of shells Holly and Kerri collected each day on their 7-day family beach vacation.

Number of Shells Collected	
Holly	5, 3, 2, 4, 0, 1, 6
Kerri	4, 6, 3, 4, 7, 5, 6

Which statement is true?

   F The mean of Holly's shells is the same as the mean of Kerri's number of shells.

   G The number of Holly's number of shells varied more from day to day than the number of Kerri's number of shells.

   H The mean of Holly's number of shells is greater than the mean of Kerri's number of shells.

   J The range of Holly's number of shells is the same as the range of Kerri's number of shells.

45. The data show the number of paintings each student has completed in art class. What is the most common number of paintings among the students in the class?

Number of Paintings				
4	7	1	3	5
4	3	7	2	2
1	2	1	6	1
1	5	2	2	2

   A 7 paintings

   B 5 paintings

   C 1 painting

   D 2 paintings

46. Kendra asked her friends how many pets they each had in their family. Her results are shown below.

4, 2, 1, 1, 0, 2, 7, 3, 1, 0, 0

Which frequency table represents the data?

F

Pets	0–1	2–3	4–5	6–7
Frequency	3	2	1	0

G

Pets	0–1	2–3	4–5	6–7
Frequency	5	2	1	1

H

Pets	0–1	2–3	4–5	6–7
Frequency	6	3	1	1

J

Pets	0–1	2–3	4–5	6–7
Frequency	6	2	1	1

47. What was the likely means of measurement for the data set shown?

Distance Driven Daily for a Week (miles)						
45	56	31	47	52	103	124

A measuring tape

B odometer

C yardstick

D ruler

48. Brianna goes to dinner with 3 of her friends. The costs of their meals are $10.00, $8.00, $11.00, and $15.00. If they split the bill evenly, how much should each person pay?

F $6.00

G $8.00

H $11.00

J $15.00

49. The histogram shows the amount of monthly allowance for the students in Melinda's class.

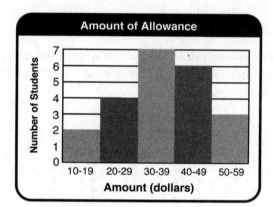

Which interval of dollar amounts represents the peak of the histogram?

A 10–19

B 20–29

C 30–39

D 40–49

50. The number of minutes Josh runs each day for 6 days are 26, 38, 33, 20, 3, and 28. What is the outlier in the data set?

   F   38

   G   27

   H   25

   J   3

Ratio and Proportion

Modeled Instruction

DIRECTIONS: Read each question and choose the best answer. Use the answer sheet provided at the end of the workbook to record your answers. If the correct answer is not available, mark the letter for "Not Here."

1. For every 2 apples in a fruit basket, there are 3 oranges. What is the ratio of apples to oranges?

A	3 to 2	C	2 to 5
B	2 to 3	D	3 to 5

 Hint

You can make a model to show a ratio. The language indicates, "2 to 3" is the ratio of apples to oranges; "3 to 2" is the ratio of oranges to apples.

2. Mr. Johnson planted 1 purple tulip for every 4 yellow tulips. How many yellow tulips will he plant if he plants 5 purple tulips?

F	20 tulips	H	6 tulips
G	25 tulips	J	5 tulips

 Hint

You can model this ratio with a table.

Purple tulips	1	2	3	4	5
Yellow tulips	4	8	12	16	□

3. Which model shows the ratio of 2 circles to 4 squares?

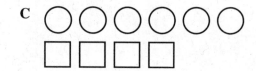

 Hint

The order in which the ratio is presented is "2 to 4." Look for that order in the models.

4. Ting is making a necklace that has 5 white beads for every 1 gold bead. Which number completes the table to show the number of white beads for 10 gold beads?

White Beads	5	10	15	20	25	30	35	40	45	□
Gold Beads	1	2	3	4	5	6	7	8	9	10

F 47   **G** 48   **H** 49   **J** 50

Hint

Look for a pattern in the table. While the bottom row of the table increases by 1, the top row of the table increases by 5.

---

5. Which of the following is a unit ratio?

A the ratio of peanuts to cashews is 12 to 4   **C** 3 daisies for each rose

B 4 cups of water for every 2 cups of rice   **D** 3 out of every 6 apples are green

Hint

A unit rate or unit ratio is a comparison where one of the numbers is 1. Look for language such as "for each" or "per."

6. In every classroom in Jackson Middle School, there are 2 closets. How many closets are in 4 classrooms?

   F 2 closets

   G 4 closets

   H 6 closets

   J 8 closets

 Hint

You can write a ratio as a fraction.

$\dfrac{1 \text{ classroom}}{2 \text{ closets}}$

Then multiply the numerator and denominator by the same number to show 4 classrooms.

$\dfrac{1 \times 4}{2 \times 4}$

7. Henry paid $2.52 for 12 ounces of crackers. What is the unit rate?

   A $\dfrac{\$0.21}{1 \text{ ounce}}$

   B $\dfrac{\$2.52}{12 \text{ ounces}}$

   C $\dfrac{\$4.76}{1 \text{ ounce}}$

   D $\dfrac{\$30.24}{12 \text{ ounces}}$

 Hint

Unit rate means how much did Henry pay for 1 ounce. You can divide to find an equivalent ratio.

$\dfrac{\$2.52}{12} \div \dfrac{12}{12} = \square$

Divide 12 ounces by 12 to get to 1 ounce. You divide $2.52 by 12 to find the unit price.

8. A recipe calls for 3 teaspoons of rice vinegar to 4 teaspoons of honey. Based on this information, which of the following statements is true?

   F The recipe has a ratio of $\dfrac{3}{4}$ teaspoons of vinegar to $\dfrac{3}{4}$ teaspoon of honey.

   G The recipe has a ratio of 1 teaspoon of vinegar to each teaspoon of honey.

   H The recipe has a ratio of $\dfrac{3}{4}$ teaspoon of honey to each teaspoon of vinegar.

   J The recipe has a ratio of $\dfrac{3}{4}$ teaspoons of vinegar to each teaspoon of honey.

 Hint

You can find the unit rate by writing the ratio as a fraction. $\dfrac{3 \text{ teaspoons rice vinegar}}{4 \text{ teaspoons honey}}$ Dividing the numerator and denominator by 4 results in an equivalent fractions with a denominator of 1.

9. This table shows equivalent ratios for granola bars that are packed at the factory. What is the unit rate in this table?

Bars	10	20	30	40
Boxes	1	2	3	4

A $\dfrac{40 \text{ bars}}{4 \text{ boxes}}$

B $\dfrac{30 \text{ bars}}{3 \text{ boxes}}$

C $\dfrac{20 \text{ bars}}{2 \text{ boxes}}$

D $\dfrac{10 \text{ bars}}{1 \text{ box}}$

 Hint

A unit rate always has 1 as a part of the ratio.

10. Dylan hikes 90 miles in 3 days. At that rate, how many days does it take him to hike a total of 240 miles?

F 8 days

G 12 days

H 15 days

J 19 days

 Hint

Start by writing the ratio as a fraction. Then set up a proportion.

11. The graph shows the amount of money Juanita earns from her tutoring job. How much does Juanita earn for 5 hours of tutoring?

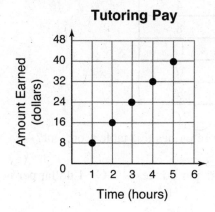

A $40.00

B $32.00

C $16.00

D $8.00

 Hint

Look for the point on the graph where the number 5 on the *x*-axis intersects the *y*-axis.

Use the table to answer questions 12 and 13.

Ounces	Dollars
1	4
2	8
3	12
4	16
5	20

12. What unit rate does this table represent?

    F 4 dollars per ounce   **G** 1 dollar per ounce   **H** 4 ounces per dollar   **J** 1 ounce per dollar

Hint

Find two numbers in the table where one of the numbers is a 1. 1 ounce for 4 dollars can be turned around. The word "per" means for each.

---

13. Which graph below represents the rate table above?

A

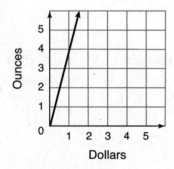

C

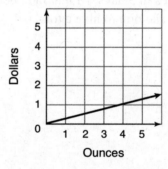

B

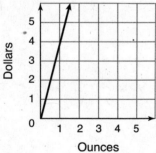

D

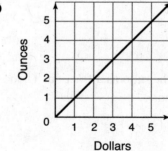

Hint

Ounces is the independent variable because the more ounces you buy the greater the cost will be. The cost is dependent on the number of ounces, so ounces are on the *x*-axis and dollars are on the *y*-axis. Look for a section of the line that intersects with 1 and 4.

14. If 5 bags of apples weigh 40 pounds, how many pounds do 2 bags of apples weigh?

F 7 pounds

G 10 pounds

H 16 pounds

J 70 pounds

Hint

You can use a tape diagram to figure out the weight of 1 bag. Each bag weighs 8 lb because $5 \times 8 = 40$.

8 lb	8 lb	8 lb	8 lb	8 lb

15. Jake collects 12 new coins each year. Use this table to decide how many coins Jake will have after 5 years.

Coins	12	24	36	48	☐
Year	1	2	3	4	5

A 49 coins

B 50 coins

C 60 coins

D 108 coins

Hint

You can see that the number of coins increases at a constant rate. Look for a pattern to see what the number of coins will be in the fifth year.

16. A 12-ounce box of Wheat-Os costs $4.08. What is the unit price per ounce?

F $\dfrac{\$0.34}{1 \text{ oz}}$

G $\dfrac{12 \text{ oz}}{1 \text{ oz}}$

H $\dfrac{\$4.08}{12 \text{ oz}}$

J Not Here

Hint

The unit price for this problem is "per ounce." Write the ratio $\dfrac{\$4.08}{12 \text{ oz}}$ as a fraction. Divide the numerator and denominator by the same number to determine the unit price.

17. A sprinting cheetah covered a distance of 518 meters in 18.5 seconds. How fast was the cheetah running?

A 30 meters per second

B 28 meters per second

C 25 meters per second

D 22 meters per second

Hint

Simplify the problem to find a solution path. If the cheetah sprinted 10 meters in 2 seconds, you could divide 10 by 2 to see that it would sprint 5 meters in 1 second. Use a similar procedure with the numbers 518 meters and 18.5 seconds.

18. What value completes the ratio table?

Recipe	
50 grams	3 eggs
25 grams	□

F $1\frac{1}{2}$ eggs

G 6 eggs

H 5 eggs

J 4 eggs

Hint

You need to write an equivalent ratio for this problem. $\frac{50}{3} = \frac{25}{\square}$

By what number do you divide 50 to get a result of 25? Divide 3 by that same number.

19. Hirva earned $60.00. She put 50% in a savings account. How much did she save?

A $10.00

B $25.00

C $30.00

D $50.00

Hint

You can use a double number line to represent the situation.

dollars   0   _____   60

percent   0%   50%   100%

What number is halfway between 0 and 60?

20. The sixth graders at Jamal's school voted for the location of their class trip. The table shows the results. If 126 students voted for going to the art museum, how many sixth graders are at Jamal's school?

Class Trip Votes	
Location	**Percent**
History museum	25%
Art museum	35%
Aquarium	40%

F 161 students

G 315 students

H 360 students

J 504 students

Hint

You can use percent notation in a ratio. Since all the percents are a multiple of 5, use 5% as the ratio unit. $\frac{126}{35\%} = \frac{\square}{5\%}$ This will give you the number of students in 5%. Once you know how many students are in 5%, you can multiply by 20 to find the total number of students.

21. A train is traveling from Orlando, Florida to Atlanta, Georgia. So far, it has traveled 25% of the distance, or 110 miles. How far is the train ride from Orlando to Atlanta?

A   247 miles

B   255 miles

C   405 miles

D   440 miles

Hint

You can use double number lines for distance problems.

miles   0   110   ___   ___   ___

percent   0%   25%   50%   75%   100%

How could you find the number of miles in the last 3 equal parts of the diagram?

Once you know the number of miles for one section, you can find the total number of miles.

22. A bottle contains 3.5 liters of water. A second bottle contains 3,750 milliliters of water. How many more milliliters are in the larger bottle than in the smaller bottle?

F   3,500 mL

G   3,400 mL

H   250 mL

J   Not Here

Hint

You need to subtract like units of measure, so first you need to change liters to milliliters. There are 1,000 milliliters in 1 liter. So, you can multiply $3.5 \times 1,000$ before you subtract.

23. Green peppers are on sale for $1.80 per pound. How much would 2.5 pounds of green peppers cost?

A $450.00

B $4.50

C $3.60

D $2.80

Hint

The answer needs to be in dollars, so set up the multiplication problem so that pounds will be eliminated.

$$\frac{\$1.80}{1 \text{ lb}} \times 2.5 \text{ lb} = \frac{\$1.80}{1 \text{ lb}} \times \frac{2.5 \text{ lb}}{1} =$$

24. A car travels 32 miles for each gallon of gas. How many gallons of gas does it need to travel 192 miles?

   F 2 gallons

   G 4 gallons

   H 5 gallons

   J 6 gallons

Hint

You can set up a proportion to solve this problem.

$$\frac{\text{miles}}{\text{gallons}} = \frac{\text{miles}}{\text{gallons}}$$

$$\frac{32 \text{ miles}}{1 \text{ gallon}} = \frac{192 \text{ miles}}{n}$$

Now solve the proportion.

25. A downhill skier is traveling at a rate of 0.5 kilometer per minute. How far will the skier travel in 18 minutes?

   A 9 kilometers

   B 18 kilometers

   C 32 kilometers

   D 36 kilometers

Hint

You can use the distance formula to solve this problem.

$$d = r \times t$$

$$d = \frac{0.5 \text{ mi}}{1 \text{ min}} \times 18 \text{ min}$$

$$d = \square$$

Ratio and Proportion

Independent Practice

DIRECTIONS: Read each question and choose the best answer. Use the answer sheet provided at the end of the workbook to record your answers. If the correct answer is not available, mark the letter for "Not Here."

26. Amelia has 7 pairs of black pants, 4 pairs of blue jeans, 3 pairs of brown pants, and 1 pair of white pants. What is the ratio of the pairs of black pants to the total number of pairs of pants?

    F   4 to 15

    G   7 to 15

    H   4 to 3

    J   1 to 3

27. For every team competing in a math competition, there are 6 students. How many students are on 3 teams?

    A   1 student

    B   9 students

    C   12 students

    D   18 students

28. At Hilltop Bakery, muffins are sold at a rate of $6.00 for 1 dozen. Which ratio gives the cost for 4 dozen muffins?

    F $12.00 : 1 dozen

    G $12.00 : 3 dozen

    H $18.00 : 4 dozen

    J $24.00 : 4 dozen

29. Jacob has 4 games. Laura has 1 game. What model shows the ratio of the number of Jacob's games to the number of Laura's games?

30. Lee uses 3 tablespoons of juice for each smoothie that she prepares. Which model could be used to describe the ratio of tablespoons of juice to the number of smoothies?

    F   3 tablespoons to 1 smoothie

    G   2 tablespoons to 1 smoothie

    H   4 tablespoons to 1 smoothie

    J   2 tablespoons to 4 smoothies

31. Brent has 8 posters, 3 photographs, 5 drawings, and 6 postcards in his room. What is the ratio of drawings to posters?

    A   5:22

    B   5:8

    C   6:5

    D   8:3

32. Dora used the grocery ads to list orange prices at four stores.

Farmer's	4 pounds for $3.32
Greenwise	2 pounds for $1.62
Fine Grocery	3 pounds for $2.37
Tosko	5 pounds for $4.50

Which store charges the least amount per pound?

F Farmer's   **H** Fine Grocery

G Greenwise   **J** Tosko

33. Robert compared the cost of scrapbook paper at 4 stores.

Scrapbook World	12 sheets for $15.61
Colorful Creations	14 sheets for $17.78
Greenview Art Supplies	15 sheets for $21.75
Artistic Memories	20 sheets for $23.00

Which store charges the least amount per sheet?

A Scrapbook World

B Greenview Art Supplies

C Artistic Memories

D Colorful Creations

34. Daniel bought 28 ounces of pretzels for $3.92. What is the unit rate per ounce?

F $\dfrac{\$0.14}{1\ \text{ounce}}$

G $\dfrac{\$3.92}{28\ \text{ounces}}$

H $\dfrac{\$7.14}{1\ \text{ounce}}$

J $\dfrac{\$109.71}{28\ \text{ounces}}$

35. The graph shows the rate at which a helicopter travels over time.

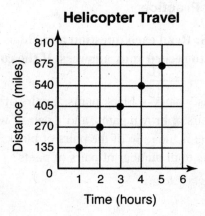

Helicopter Travel

How far will the helicopter travel in 8 hours?

A 945 miles

B 1,080 miles

C 1,215 miles

D Not Here

36. Kelsey can make 2 loaves of bread with 6 cups of flour. How many loaves of bread can she make with 24 cups of flour?

F 4 loaves

G 8 loaves

H 12 loaves

J 36 loaves

37. The table shows the hockey standings for teams in an intramural league.

Hockey Standings		
Team	**Wins**	**Losses**
Stars	10	15
Penguins	15	10
Wildcats	12	8
Bears	8	10

Which hockey teams have equivalent ratios of wins to losses?

A Penguins and Wildcats

B Wildcats and Stars

C Bears and Wildcats

D Bears and Stars

38. Mr. Franklin's class has 12 boys and 14 girls. Which ratio is equivalent to $\frac{12}{14}$?

F $\frac{12}{26}$

G $\frac{6}{7}$

H $\frac{5}{6}$

J $\frac{2}{3}$

39. Kevin burns 75 calories for every 15 minutes he rides his bicycle. At that rate, how many calories will Kevin burn if he rides his bicycle for 90 minutes?

A 12.5 calories

B 225 calories

C 375 calories

D 450 calories

40. Which ratio is equivalent to $\frac{8}{24}$?

F $\frac{4}{24}$

G $\frac{6}{24}$

H $\frac{4}{12}$

J $\frac{12}{28}$

41. There are 12 red bicycles and 21 blue bicycles available for rent. Which ratio is equivalent to $\frac{12}{21}$?

A $\frac{4}{7}$

B $\frac{12}{33}$

C $\frac{9}{21}$

D $\frac{2}{7}$

42. The number of comedy and action films that 4 friends saw during the year is recorded in the table.

Films for the Year		
Friend	**Comedy**	**Action**
William	8	12
Kia	3	11
Ricardo	10	15
Shawnda	12	5

Which 2 friends saw equivalent ratios of comedy films to action films?

F William and Kia

G William and Ricardo

H Ricardo and Shawnda

J Kia and Shawnda

43. The table shows the numbers of calories in 4 ounces of several types of fruit juice.

Calories in 4 Ounces of Juice	
Type of Juice	**Calories**
Orange	56
Apple	60
Grape	76

How many calories are there in 7 ounces of orange juice?

A 98 calories

B 105 calories

C 133 calories

D 392 calories

44. On a map of a hiking trail, 2 inches represent 5 miles. The map distance from the beginning of the trail to Sky Falls is 4 inches. What is the actual distance, in miles, from the beginning of the trail to Sky Falls?

F 22 miles

G 20 miles

H 10 miles

J 8 miles

45. If 7 bags of flour weigh 35 pounds, how many pounds do 15 bags of flour weigh?

A 5 pounds

B 20 pounds

C 75 pounds

D 105 pounds

46. Michael has visited 40 museums in Illinois and Indiana. Twenty percent of the museums were in Indiana. How many more museums did he visit in Illinois than in Indiana?

F 8 museums

G 18 museums

H 20 museums

J 24 museums

47. Malik was paid $30.00 each week to help his neighbor with yard work during the summer. He saves 35% of the money he earns. How much does Malik save each week?

A $1.05

B $10.50

C $19.50

D $22.50

48. The Mills Times reported that $\frac{7}{10}$ of residents voted in the city election. What percent of residents voted?

F 700

G 70%

H 7%

J 0.7%

49. Which percent represents the shaded part?

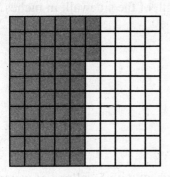

A 53%

B 35%

C 5.3%

D 3.5%

50. Which fraction is equivalent to 272%?

F $\dfrac{272}{1,000}$

G $\dfrac{272}{10}$

H $\dfrac{136}{50}$

J $\dfrac{136}{5}$

51. How is the decimal 2.4 expressed as a percent?

A 0.024%

B 2.4%

C 24%

D 240%

52. Freddy has saved 65% of the money he needs to buy a new skateboard that costs $125.00. How much more does he need to save to buy the skateboard?

F $25.50

G $43.75

H $60.00

J $81.25

53. What decimal is equivalent to 2.13%?

A 0.0213

B 0.213

C 2.13

D 21.3

54. Carly is a drummer in the school band. By the end of the year, she had played in 85% of the 20 concerts the band played. In how many concerts did Carly NOT play?

F 18 concerts

G 17 concerts

H 12 concerts

J 3 concerts

55. 12 is 30% of what number?

A 18

B 36

C 40

D 400

56. A gardener spends 6 hours a week pulling weeds. How many hours does the gardener spend pulling weeds in 5 weeks?

   F   11 hours

   G   16 hours

   H   24 hours

   J   30 hours

57. A recipe calls for 3 quarts of liquid. How many cups are in 3 quarts?

   A   4 cups

   B   9 cups

   C   12 cups

   D   32 cups

58. A leaf is floating down a stream that is moving at a rate of 55 feet per minute. How far downstream does the leaf travel in 12 minutes?

   F   660 feet

   G   458 feet

   H   67 feet

   J   55 feet

59. The sidewalk at Haley's house is 5 yards long. What is the length of the sidewalk in inches?

   A   36 inches

   B   60 inches

   C   180 inches

   D   185 inches

60. Adam filled a bucket with 5 gallons of water. How many pints of water did he put in the bucket?

   F   8 pints

   G   40 pints

   H   80 pints

   J   120 pints

Number Sense

Modeled Instruction

DIRECTIONS: Read each question and choose the best answer. Use the answer sheet provided at the end of the workbook to record your answers. If the correct answer is not available, mark the letter for "Not Here."

1. Brandi made $\frac{4}{5}$ pound of trail mix and divided the mix into 4 equal portions. What is the weight of each portion?

   A $\frac{1}{10}$ pound

   B $\frac{1}{8}$ pound

   C $\frac{1}{5}$ pound

   D $\frac{1}{4}$ pound

Hint

You can use a tape diagram to visualize this problem.

1 whole pound			

$\frac{1}{5}$	$\frac{1}{5}$	$\frac{1}{5}$	$\frac{1}{5}$

$\frac{4}{5}$ pound

2. City workers are repaving a street that is $2\frac{3}{4}$ miles long. If they repave $\frac{1}{4}$ mile per day, how long will it take to repave the entire street?

   F 11 days

   G 9 days

   H 7 days

   J 5 days

Hint

Think, "How many quarter miles are there in $2\frac{3}{4}$ miles?" Because the denominators involved are 4, you can rewrite the fractions as decimals and divide.
$2.75 \div 0.25 = d$

3. Factory workers packaged 2,688 pens into 24 boxes. Each box contained the same number of pens. How many pens are in each box?

A 100 pens

B 112 pens

C 124 pens

D 136 pens

Hint

Use number sense to choose an operation. The problem tells you 2,688 was separated into 24 equal groups. When you see that each box contains the same number of pens, you should divide.

4. Tabitha's parents deposited a total amount of $6,300.00 into her college fund during a 36-month period. They deposited the same amount each month. What was their monthly contribution to Tabitha's college fund?

F $75.00

G $150.00

H $175.00

J $200.00

Hint

The problem tells you to break apart $6,300.00 into 36 equal amounts. This means you should divide.

5. Jordan is comparing the lengths of two leaves. One leaf is 3.33 centimeters long, and the other leaf is 7.01 centimeters long. What is the difference in length between the two leaves?

A 10.34 centimeters

B 6.677 centimeters

C 3.77 centimeters

D 3.68 centimeters

Hint

You subtract to find the difference between two measurements. Watch for regrouping.

6. There should be 6.14 grams of salt in a solution. If 1.8 grams of salt have been added to the solution, how many more grams of salt need to be added?

F 4.94 grams

G 4.34 grams

H 4.32 grams

J 2.34 grams

Hint

The problem asks how many more grams are needed. You can subtract to find the difference. Notice the decimals do not have the same number of decimals places, so align the numbers on the decimal point.

7. Maria works 18.5 hours each week at a shoe store. She earns $9.52 per hour. How much does Maria earn each week?

A $190.00

B $176.12

C $175.75

D $17.61

Hint

You multiply hours × salary to find total earnings. $18.5 \times \$9.52 = s$

8. A piece of land measuring 216.144 square kilometers was divided and then sold in equal parts to 12 different people. How many square kilometers did each person buy?

F 0.18012 square kilometer

G 1.8012 square kilometers

H 18.012 square kilometers

J 180.12 square kilometers

Hint

It is clear you will use division to solve this problem. Since there are so many places in the dividend, use estimation to check your answer. Look for multiples near the original numbers that are easy to divide in your head, such as 216 ÷ 12 = 18.

The answer should be close to 18.

9. What is the least common multiple (LCM) of 6 and 15?

A 6

B 15

C 30

D 60

Hint

The least common multiple, or LCM, is the least (smallest) number that two or more numbers have in common in their list of nonzero multiples. Why can't 6 or 15 be the least common multiple in this case?

10. What is the GCF (Greatest Common Factor) of 18 and 45?

F 45

G 18

H 15

J 9

Hint

A common factor is a number that is a factor of two or more numbers. The greatest common factor, or GCF, is the greatest factor that two or more numbers have in common.

Number Sense
Higher Scores on Math, Grade 6

11. Which equation uses the Distributive Property to express the sum of 9 and 27 as a product?

A $9 + 27 = 9(1 + 3)$

B $9 + 27 = 27 + 9$

C $9 + 27 = 36$

D $9 + 27 = 9 \times 2 + 18$

Hint

Write each number as the product of the GCF (Greatest Common Factor) and another factor. The GCF is 9.

$9 = 9 \times 1$ $27 = 9 \times 3$

Look for an equation multiplying the GCF and the sum of the two factors.

12. Which situation could be represented by the integer $+13$?

F A city is 13 feet above sea level.

G A football team loses 13 yards on a play.

H A withdrawal of $13.00 is made from a bank account.

J A student answers 13 items incorrectly.

Hint

Positive numbers are always greater than, or above, 0. Sea level is generally considered to be at 0.

13. What is the opposite of -4?

A -4

B 0

C 4

D Not Here

Hint

Think of a number line. Opposite numbers are the same distance from 0.

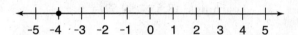

14. Which expression has the same value as $-(-6)$?

F 0

G $6 - 6$

H 6

J -6

Hint

You should read this expression as "the opposite of negative 6." It is easier to see that the opposite of a negative number is positive.

15. A baseball stadium is represented by the point $(-3, -5)$ on a coordinate plane. In which quadrant does the point lie?

A Quadrant I

B Quadrant II

C Quadrant III

D Quadrant IV

Hint

Visualize a coordinate plane to answer this question. You start counting quadrants with the top right quadrant.

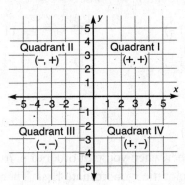

16. Which two points are reflected across the *y*-axis?

F $(2, 4)$ and $(-2, 4)$

G $(2, 4)$ and $(4, -2)$

H $(2, 4)$ and $(-4, -2)$

J Not Here

Hint

Two points are reflections of each other if the *x*-axis or *y*-axis forms a line of symmetry for the two points. Think about the signs of the integers in each quadrant.

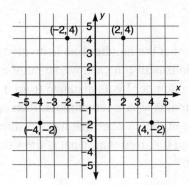

Name _____   Date _____

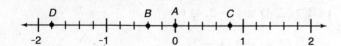

17. What decimal represents the value of point *B*?

A   −0.1

B   −0.2

C   −0.3

D   −0.4

Hint

Notice that the number line is divided into 5 sections between each whole number. You name a number by its distance from 0. Since a decimal is a base ten number, then each section of the number line has a distance of 0.2 from 0. Given that, what is the value of point *B*?

18. What fraction represents the value of point *C*?

F $\frac{4}{5}$

G $-\frac{4}{5}$

H $\frac{1}{5}$

J $-\frac{1}{5}$

Hint

The number line has 5 sections between each whole number. Since the question asks for a fraction, then each section has a value of $\frac{1}{5}$. Given that, what is the value of point *C*?

Use this coordinate plane for questions 19 and 20 below.

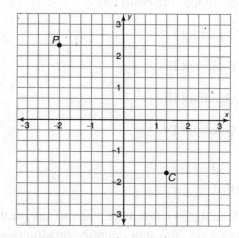

19. What is the location of point *C*?

A $(1\frac{1}{3}, -1\frac{2}{3})$ C $(-1\frac{1}{3}, 11\frac{2}{3})$

B $(1\frac{2}{3}, -1\frac{1}{3})$ D $(-1\frac{2}{3}, 1\frac{1}{3})$

Hint

Remember when you plot ordered pairs, you always plot the *x*-coordinate first. Then you plot the *y*-coordinate. You read the location of the points the same way: *x*-coordinate first, then *y*-coordinate. Notice that the scale is set up for fractions and mixed numbers that include thirds.

20. What is the location of point *P*?

F $(2\frac{1}{3}, -2)$ H $(-2, -2\frac{1}{3})$

G $(\frac{2}{3}, 2\frac{1}{3})$ J $(-2, 2\frac{1}{3})$

Hint

The points on the scale of the coordinate plane allow for mixed numbers to be plotted. All the points on the scale are not labeled. Remember to read the *x*-coordinate first.

21. Which list shows these integers in order from least to greatest?

3, −7, 0, 4, −1

A   0, −1, 3, 4, −7

B   −7, −1, 0, 3, 4

C   4, 3, 0, −1, −7

D   3, 4, 0, −1, −7

Hint

You can use a number line to help you compare.

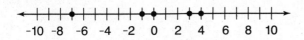

-10 -8 -6 -4 -2 0 2 4 6 8 10

On a number line, the numbers to the right of 0 are positive numbers. They become greater as you move to the right. The numbers to the left of 0 are negative numbers. They become lesser (smaller) as you move to the left.

22. The wind-chill temperatures on Tuesday for four cities are −8.2°F, −7.7°F, −5.8°F, and −6.2°F. Which list shows these numbers in order from greatest to least?

F   −8.2°F, −7.7°F, −5.8°F, −6.2°F

G   −5.8°F, −6.2°F, −7.7°F, −8.2°F,

H   −8.2°F, −7.7°F, −6.2°F, −5.8°F

J   −6.2°F, −5.8°F, −7.7°F, −8.2°F

Hint

Remember that with negative numbers, the greater the number the lesser its value.
So, −8.2 is less than −5.8.

23. A shipwreck was spotted at a depth of 275 ft. What is the shipwreck's actual distance from sea level?

A   −275 ft

B |−275 ft|

C   2 × 75 ft

D   Not Here

Hint

The absolute value is a measure of distance from 0. The distance between two points can never be negative, so, absolute value is never a negative number.

$|275| = 275$ $|−275| = 275$

24. What symbol will make this inequality true?

$\frac{1}{4}$ ◯ $|−2.4|$

F   >

G   <

H   =

J   +

Hint

When you see absolute value symbols, look at the face value of the number. In this case you are comparing $\frac{1}{4}$ and 2.4.

25. Zachary has graphed the location of the middle school at $(-6, 5)$. He has graphed the high school 3 units to the right of the middle school. What is the high school's ordered pair?

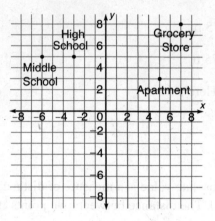

A $(-3, 5)$

B $(3, 5)$

C $(5, 3)$

D $(-3, -5)$

 Hint

Find the point for the high school on the grid.

You read the location of a point the same way you plot a point.

Read the *x*-coordinate first and the *y*-coordinate second.

Number Sense

Independent Practice

DIRECTIONS: Read each question and choose the best answer. Use the answer sheet provided at the end of the workbook to record your answers. If the correct answer is not available, mark the letter for "Not Here."

26. How many $\frac{2}{3}$-cup servings are in an 8-cup container of juice?

    F $5\frac{1}{3}$

    G 6

    H 12

    J 16

27. Yancy has a board 25 feet long. He wants to cut the board into $4\frac{1}{2}$ foot lengths. Into how many $4\frac{1}{2}$-foot lengths can he cut it?

    A 2

    B 4

    C 5

    D 6

28. Joseph buys 3 pounds of hamburger. How many quarter-pound hamburgers can he make?

    F $\frac{3}{4}$ hamburger

    G $1\frac{1}{2}$ hamburgers

    H 12 hamburgers

    J 16 hamburgers

29. Divide. Express your answer in simplest form.

    $6\frac{1}{4} \div 3\frac{1}{20}$

    A $2\frac{1}{10}$

    B $2\frac{3}{61}$

    C $2\frac{7}{72}$

    D $18\frac{1}{24}$

30. Find the quotient. Express your answer in simplest form.

    $1\frac{1}{4} \div \frac{3}{8}$

    F $\frac{3}{4}$

    G $\frac{3}{8}$

    H $2\frac{1}{4}$

    J $3\frac{1}{3}$

31. The 134 sixth-grade students sit together in the auditorium. Each row has 12 seats. How many rows do the sixth graders need?

    A $10\frac{5}{6}$ rows

    B $11\frac{1}{6}$ rows

    C 132 rows

    D 146 rows

32. Jean writes 217 pages in her journal in 31 days. What is the average number of pages she writes each day?

F 7 pages

G 31 pages

H 186 pages

J 248 pages

33. Find the quotient.

$2{,}263 \div 26$

A 2,289

B 2,237

C $87\frac{1}{26}$

D $26\frac{1}{87}$

34. Stella works three afternoons per week at a local flower shop. She earns $35.00 per day. How many weeks will Stella have to work in order to earn $525.00?

F 3 weeks

G 5 weeks

H 9 weeks

J 10 weeks

35. Use the rate schedule.

Electric Rate Schedule	
First 2,000 kWh	$0.053 per kWh
Over 2,000 kWh	$0.04 per kWh

Delsin runs a small bookstore. Last month his store used 8,000 kWh of electricity. What was his bill?

A $375.00

B $346.00

C $320.00

D $240.00

36. Jorge is building a table out of boards that are 3.75 inches wide. He wants the table to be at least 36 inches wide. How many boards does he need?

F 9 boards

G 9.6 boards

H 10 boards

J 135 boards

37. Solve.

$26 - 0.7$

A 26.7

B 26.3

C 25.7

D 25.3

38. Solve.

$3.57 + 1.29$

F   2.28

G   4.86

H   6.48

J   10.64

39. A surveyor marks off 15 small adjacent lots each 0.1 mile wide. What is the total width in miles?

A   1 mile

B   1.25 miles

C   1.5 miles

D   15 miles

40. An oak tree is 15 meters tall. The tree next to it is 12.38 meters tall. What is the difference between the heights of the trees?

F   2.62 meters

G   13.762 meters

H   27.38 meters

J   Not Here

41. A bag of hot dog buns contains 8 buns, and a package of hot dogs contains 10 hot dogs. How many packages of each are needed so that each of the 40 campers has a hot dog and a bun with none left over?

A   8 bags of buns, 10 packages of hot dogs

B   5 bags of buns, 4 packages of hot dogs

C   4 bags of buns, 5 packages of hot dogs

D   2 bags of buns, 2 packages of hot dogs

42. $4 \times 32 = (4 \times 30) + (4 \times 2)$ is an example of which property?

F   Commutative Property

G   Distributive Property

H   Associative Property

J   Exponential Property

43. What is the greatest common factor of 42 and 66?

A   72

B   6

C   3

D   2

44. What is the least common multiple of 12 and 8?

F   12

G   16

H   24

J   48

45. Which gives $28 + 24$ as a product of the GCF and a sum?

A $40 + 12$

B $2(14 + 12)$

C $2(26 + 22)$

D $4(7 + 6)$

46. Stacy's thermostat is set at 74°F. Which range of numbers contains the opposite of Stacy's thermostat setting?

    F   60 to 80

    G   −80 to −60

    H   −30 to −20

    J   −10 to −10

47. Which number best represents the situation, "A plane descends 1,300 ft"?

    A   1,300

    B   13

    C   −1,300

    D   −13

48. Which situation would NOT be represented by a negative integer?

    F   an increase of 6 pounds

    G   a loss of $45.00

    H   a decrease of 12 yards

    J   4 inches below normal

49. What is the opposite of the integer on the number line? Assume that each tick mark represents 1 unit.

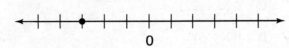

    A   3

    B   −3

    C   6

    D   −6

50. Which number added to −243 gives the sum of +243?

    F   −243

    G   243

    H   −486

    J   486

51. What integer and its opposite are represented by this graph?

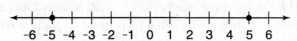

    A   −4, 5

    B   −5, 5

    C   −5, 6

    D   −6, 6

52. In what quadrant is point *B* located?

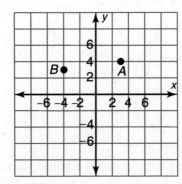

    F   Quadrant I

    G   Quadrant II

    H   Quadrant III

    J   Quadrant IV

Name _____   Date _____

53. Name the quadrant of the coordinate plane where the point $(4, -2)$ is located.

   A Quadrant I

   B Quadrant II

   C Quadrant III

   D Quadrant IV

54. Which statement about the coordinates of a figure reflected across the y-axis is true?

   F The y-coordinates will have opposite signs.

   G Both the x- and y-coordinates will have opposite signs.

   H The x-coordinates will have opposite signs.

   J Both the x- and y-coordinates will remain the same.

55. The coordinates of three vertices of a rectangle are $A(2, -5)$, $B(2, 3)$, and $C(10, 3)$. Find the coordinates of the fourth vertex D.

   A $D(10, 1)$

   B $D(10, -5)$

   C $D(1, 10)$

   D $D(-5, 10)$

56. Which points share the same y-coordinate?

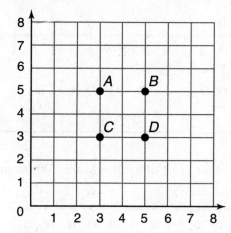

   F A and C

   G B and D

   H C and B

   J C and D

57. What is the ordered pair of your location if you start at $(0, 0)$, move 4 units up, and then move 3 units right?

   A $(3, 4)$

   B $(4, 3)$

   C $(-3, 4)$

   D $(3, -4)$

58. Use the number line to list points *A*, *B*, *C*, and *D* from greatest to least.

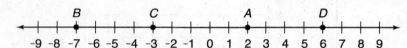

    F   *A, B, C, D*   **G**   *D, A, C, B*   **H**   *C, A, B, D*   **J**   *B, C, A, D*

---

59. Terrell is four years older than Malik. Which number line shows the possible ages of Terrel, *T*, and Malik, *M*?

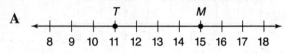

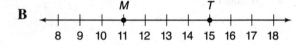

---

60. Micah wrote the following list of numbers: −2.3, −4.6, −5.9, and 1.4. Which list shows the numbers arranged from greatest to least?

    F   −5.9, −2.3, −4.6, 1.4   **H**   −5.9, −4.6, −2,3, 1.4

    G   1.4, −2.3, −5.9, −4.6   **J**   1.4, −2.3, −4.6, −5.9

---

61. According to the table, when was the temperature the coldest?

Time	Temperature (°F)
9:00 P.M.	8
Midnight	5
3:00 A.M.	−1
6:00 A.M.	−6

    A   9:00 P.M.   **B**   midnight   **C**   3:00 A.M.   **D**   6:00 A.M.

62. List these numbers in order from least to greatest.

$\frac{5}{8}, -0.25, -\frac{1}{8}, 1.5$

F $\frac{5}{8}, -0.25, -\frac{1}{8}, 1.5$

G $1.5, -\frac{1}{8}, -0.25, \frac{5}{8}$

H $1.5, \frac{5}{8}, -0.25, -\frac{1}{8}$

J, $-0.25, -\frac{1}{8}, \frac{5}{8}, 1.5$

63. What is $|-27|$?

A -27

B 0

C 1

D 27

64. Which is NOT equal to the absolute value of -61?

F $|61|$

G $-|61|$

H $|-61|$

J 61

65. Simplify $-|-2|$?

A -2

B 2

C $\frac{1}{2}$

D 1

66. Which inequality best represents the following statement?

The city is located more than 2,000 feet above sea level.

F $c > 2,000$

G $c < 2,000$

H $c < -2,000$

J Not Here

67. While scuba diving, Renee explored the ocean at an elevation of -20 feet. Sam was closer to the surface of the water than Renee. Which describes Sam's depth?

A an elevation greater than -20 feet

B an elevation greater than 20 feet

C an elevation less than -20 feet

D Not Here

68. Which inequality represents the graph below?

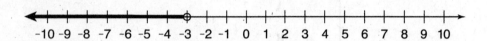

F $x < -3$ **G** $x > -3$ **H** $x \le -3$ **J** $x \ge -3$

---

69. Find the perimeter of the rectangle.

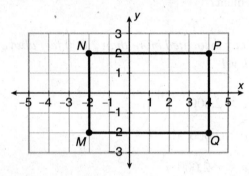

A The perimeter of the rectangle is 10 units.

B The perimeter of the rectangle is 16 units.

C The perimeter of the rectangle is 20 units.

D The perimeter of the rectangle is 24 units.

---

70. Which graph shows a line through the ordered pairs $(1, -1), (2, 1), (0, -3), (-1, -5)$?

F
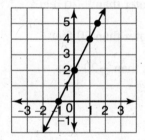

H
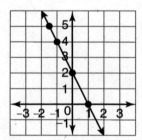

G
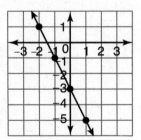

J
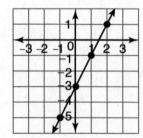

71. In what quadrant is the point $(-7, -2)$ located?

   A Quadrant I

   B Quadrant II

   C Quadrant III

   D Quadrant IV

72. Each unit on the coordinate plane represents 1 mile. How far is the grocery store from the dry cleaners?

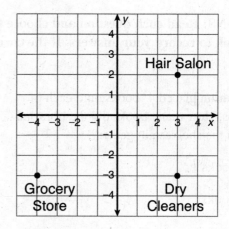

   F 5 miles

   G 7 miles

   H 8 miles

   J 14 miles

Expressions and Equations

Modeled Instruction

DIRECTIONS: Read each question and choose the best answer. Use the answer sheet provided at the end of the workbook to record your answers. If the correct answer is not available, mark the letter for "Not Here."

1. The librarian placed 4^2 books onto each of 5 shelves. How many books did the librarian place on the shelves altogether?

   A 80 books

   B 25 books

   C 20 books

   D 16 books

   Hint

   In the number 4^2, the exponent is 2 and 4 is the base. The exponent tells how many times a number is used as a factor. The base is the number being multiplied repeatedly.

   $4^2 = 4 \times 4 = \square$

   Find the number of books she placed on each shelf. Then multiply by 5 to find the total.

2. Which expression has a value of 4?

   F $7 + (2^2 - 3) + 4 \times 4$

   G $3 \times (7^2 - 4) \times 4 + 2$

   H $4^2 + 3 \times (7 - 2) + 4$

   J $2^2 \times 7 - (4 + 4) \times 3$

   Hint

   Remember to apply the Order of Operations when simplifying an expression.
   1) Parentheses
   2) Exponents
   3) Multiply and Divide from Left to Right
   4) Add and Subtract from Left to Right

3. There are 16 ounces in 1 pound. Which expression gives the number of ounces in p pounds?

A $16p$

B $p \div 16$

C $16 + p$

D $16 - p$

Hint

In mathematics, it is assumed that the p actually means $1p$ and it is not necessary to write the 1. For this reason, we can write $16p$ and it means $16 \times 1p$. This formula allows you to multiply 16 times any number of pounds to find the number of ounces in that number of pounds.

4. The length of a swimming pool is 5 feet shorter than twice the width. Let n represent the width. Which expression gives the length of the swimming pool?

F $2n + 5$

G $2n - 5$

H $2(n - 5)$

J $2(n + 5)$

Hint

You know that n represents the width. The width is 2 times the width minus 5. Replace the word width with n to decide on the correct expression.

5. How many terms does this expression have?

$2e - \int$

A 4

B 3

C 2

D 1

Hint

The terms of an expression are separated by a plus sign or a minus sign.

6. Which of the following describes a part in this expression?

$(12 \times 6) + (4 \times 8) - 7$

F the difference of 8 and 7

G the sum of 6 and 4

H the quotient of 4 and 8

J the product of 12 and 6

Hint

You must always work inside the parentheses before other operations. Once you have multiplied the factors inside the parentheses, then you can add and subtract from left to right.

Name _____ Date _____

7. What is the volume of a cube with a side length of $\frac{1}{2}$ in.?

A $\frac{1}{8}$ cubic inch

B $\frac{1}{8}$ inch

C $1\frac{1}{2}$ cubic centimeters

D $1\frac{1}{2}$ centimeters

Hint

You can use the formula $V = s^3$ to find the volume of a cube. This formula means $s \times s \times s$. You can use s^3 because all the faces of a cube have the same side length.

8. The expression $180(n - 2)$ gives the sum of the measures of the angles, in degrees, of a polygon with n sides. What is the sum of the measures of the angles in a polygon with 10 sides?

F 1,080 degrees

G 1,440 degrees

H 1,880 degrees

J 2,160 degrees

Hint

When a number is placed directly outside a set of parentheses, it means that you must multiply that number times the result in the parentheses.

9. Nicolás bought a pair of sandals for $27.00, four shirts, and a jacket for $54.00. To find the total cost in dollars, he wrote $27 + 4s + 54 = 27 + 54 + 4s$. Which property does the equation show?

A Identity Property of 1

B Distributive Property of Multiplication over Addition

C Associative Property of Addition

D Commutative Property of Addition

Hint

The Commutative Property of Addition states that changing the order of the addends does not change the sum. The Associative Property of Addition states that moving the grouping symbols of an addition expression does not change the sum.

10. An artist bought p large tubes of paint for $25.00 each and p small tubes of paint for $15.00 each. The expression $p \times 25 + p \times 15$ gives the total cost, in dollars, of the tubes of paint. Which shows another way to write this expression?

F $p(25 + 15)$

G $p(25 \times 15)$

H $p(25 \times p) + 15$

J $p(25 + p)15$

Hint

The letter p represents the number of each item that was bought. You can see that p is to be multiplied by both 25 and 15. You can write a simpler problem by applying the Distributive Property of Multiplication over Addition.

11. Which equation uses the Distributive Property to express the sum of 45 and 54 as a product?

A $(9 \times 5) \times (9 \times 6)$

B $(4 + 5) \times (5 + 4)$

C $5(9 + 6)$

D $9(5 + 6)$

Hint

Think of a common factor of both 45 and 54. Place that common factor outside the parentheses. Then think of the other two factors and place them as a sum inside the parentheses.

12. Which expression is equivalent to $3(h + 2) - h$?

F $h + 6$

G $2h + 6$

H $h + 2$

J $2h + 2$

Hint

Begin simplifying by multiplying 3 times both h and 2. Then subtract h. Since the last h is separated by a minus sign, subtracting it will be the last step.

13. After spending $5.25 on a magazine, Terry has $16.75 left. The equation $m - 5.25 = 16.75$ can be used to find the amount of money, m, Terry had before purchasing the magazine. Which amount is a solution of the equation?

A $m = \$22.00$

B $m = \$11.50$

C $m = \$9.00$

D $m = \$8.25$

Hint

Think about working backward. Start with the money Terry had left and add the amount she spent. Check your answer by subtracting $5.25 to see if $16.75 is the amount left.

14. Motorists must travel at a speed no more than 25 miles per hour in a school zone. The inequality $s \le 25$ represents the permitted speeds. Which number is NOT a solution of the inequality?

F $s = 15$

G $s = 20$

H $s = 25$

J $s = 30$

Hint

The symbol $\le$ means "less than or equal to." This means the driving speed allowed is 25 miles per hour or less.

15. Bill must score at least 85 points on his final test to get a B in social studies. The inequality $p \geq 85$ represents the possible number of points, p, that he can score. Which number is a solution of the inequality?

A $p = 92$

B $p = 84$

C $p = 80$

D $p = 75$

 Hint

The symbol $\geq$ means "greater than or equal to." This means the score Bill makes must be equal to 85 or greater.

16. A builder needs 3 bolts to install each door. The expression $3d$ gives the number of bolts needed to install d doors. Which best describes the value of the variable d?

F a single unknown number

G any positive number

H any positive counting number

J any integer

 Hint

Think about what is included in each number description.
• A single unknown number includes negative numbers or fractions and decimals.
• Any positive number includes whole numbers, fractions, and decimals.
• Any positive counting number includes whole numbers only.
• Any integer includes negative numbers.

17. Don wrote the expression 54 less than the product of m and 15. What algebraic expression did he write? What is the value of the expression for $m = 7$?

A $54m + 15$; 393

B $15m + 54$; 159

C $15m - 54$; 51

D $54m - 15$; 363

 Hint

54 less than a product means subtract 54 from a product.

The product of m and 15 means multiply the two terms.

When you multiply m and 15, the result is a product.

18. A driver travels 150 miles in h hours. Which best describes the value of h?

F a single unknown number

G any nonnegative number

H any whole number

J any integer

 Hint

Since hours is a unit of measure, it can be measured in whole numbers, decimals, or fractions. However, it cannot be measured in negative numbers.

19. Kendra was born in 1990. Her cousin Melody was born 11 years after Kendra. Which equation could be used to find the year in which Melody was born?

A $y \times 11 = 1990$

B $y \div 11 = 1990$

C $y + 11 = 1990$

D $y - 11 = 1990$

 Hint

The most straightforward way to solve this is $1990 + 11 =$ Melody's birth year. But that is not one of the answer choices. You know that addition and subtraction are inverse operations. Thinking about that will help you find the correct option.

20. Deena adds $1\frac{2}{3}$ cups of oats to some flour to make $4\frac{3}{4}$ cups of baking mix. She solves the equation $f + 1\frac{2}{3} = 4\frac{3}{4}$ to find the amount of flour, f, in the baking mix. How much flour is in the baking mix?

F $1\frac{2}{3}$ cups   **H** $3\frac{1}{12}$ cups

G $2\frac{1}{3}$ cups   **J** $6\frac{5}{12}$ cups

 Hint

The given addition equation is the situation equation. It matches the structure of the problem. Think about how you can use an inverse operation to solve the problem.

$$f + 1\frac{2}{3} = 4\frac{3}{4}$$
$$4\frac{3}{4} - 1\frac{2}{3} = f$$

21. During a school fundraiser, Dominic sold tumblers for $12.00 each and earned a total of $324.00. Which equation could be used to find the number of tumblers, t, Dominic sold?

A $t \times 12 = 324$

B $t \div 12 = 324$

C $t + 12 = 324$

D $t - 12 = 324$

 Hint

Use the information in the problem to write a word equation.

number of tumblers $\times$ \$12.00 = total amount

22. A freight car can carry no more than 125 tons of cargo. Which inequality represents the number of tons, *t,* that the freight car can carry?

F $t < 125$

G $t > 125$

H $t \leq 125$

J $t \geq 125$

Hint

You can think of a number line.

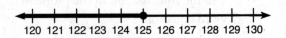

120 121 122 123 124 125 126 127 128 129 130

No more than 125 tons means 125 tons or any amount less than 125 tons.

As you move to the left on a number line, the numbers get smaller.

23. At least 10 people have to be registered for art classes at the community center, or the art classes are cancelled. Which inequality shows this situation?

A $r > 10$

B $r \geq 10$

C $r < 10$

D $r \leq 10$

Hint

At least 10 people means 10 people or more. Which symbol means equal to or greater than?

The graph below shows the cost of buying comic books from an online retailer. The shipping charge is always the same no matter how many comic books are purchased. Use the graph for questions 24 and 25.

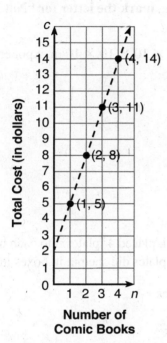

Number of Comic Books

24. What is the shipping cost?

F $5.00

G $3.00

H $2.00

J $1.00

Hint

You can see that the *y*-axis represents all costs. The line starts at $2.00 because the shipping cost is always the same.

25. Which equation represents the total cost in dollars, *c*, for *n* comic books?

A $c = 3n + 2$

B $c = 2n + 3$

C $c = 3n$

D $c = 2n$

Hint

The graph shows that 1 comic book with shipping costs $5.00. You can subtract the shipping cost to find the cost of 1 comic book. To find the total cost, you can write a word equation.

Total cost = Cost of 1 comic book × *n* (total number of comic books) + shipping cost

Expressions and Equations

Independent Practice

DIRECTIONS: Read each question and choose the best answer. Use the answer sheet provided at the end of the workbook to record your answers. If the correct answer is not available, mark the letter for "Not Here."

26. Kris sends an e-mail to 5 people, and each of those people will send the e-mail to 5 more people, and so on. Which expression shows the number of people who will have received the e-mail at the end of the third round?

 F 5×3

 G 3^5

 H 5^3

 J 3×5

27. Which expression has a value of 24?

 A $4 + 2^2$

 B $4^2 + 2^3$

 C $(4 + 2)^2$

 D $4^2 - 2^2$

28. What is the value of $6^2 - (9 - 5) \div 4$?

 F 8

 G 35

 H 39

 J 42

29. Express $10 \times 10 \times 10 \times 10$ in exponential form.

 A 4^{10}

 B 10,000

 C 10×4^4

 D 10^4

30. A store clerk placed 4^2 plates into each of 8 boxes. How many plates did she put in boxes in all?

 F 16 plates

 G 32 plates

 H 128 plates

 J 256 plates

31. Hendrick makes birdhouses. It takes him 35 minutes to make a birdhouse. What is an expression that shows how long it takes him to make t birdhouses?

 A $35 + t$

 B $35t$

 C $35 - t$

 D $35 \div t$

32. Which expression shows twelve less than a number?

   F $12 - w$

   G $12w$

   H $12 \div w$

   J $w - 12$

33. Write "3 times the sum of a number and 5" as an algebraic expression.

   A $3(n + 5)$

   B $3n + 5$

   C $3(n - 5)$

   D $3 \times 5 + n$

34. The length of a box is 7 inches more than three times its width. Let w represent the width. Which expression gives the length of the box?

   F $3w + 7$

   G $3w - 7$

   H $3(w + 7)$

   J $3(w - 7)$

35. What operation does the word "difference" indicate?

   A   addition

   B   subtraction

   C   multiplication

   D   division

36. Identify the terms in the expression $6x^2 + 14x - 12$.

   F $6x^2$, $14x$, and 12

   G   6, 14, and 12

   H x^2 and x

   J $6x^2$ and $14x$

37. Olivia's teacher asks her to write an expression that contains four terms, two exponents, and a quotient. Olivia writes the expression $3x^2 + y^3 + \frac{z}{15}$. Does her expression satisfy all the requirements? If not, describe a change she could make to create an expression that meets all the requirements.

   A   Yes, it meets the requirements.

   B   No; she could change $\frac{z}{15}$ in her expression to $z + 15$.

   C   No; she could change $3x^2$ in her expression to $3(x^2)$.

   D   No; she could subtract the term $2n$ from her expression.

38. Simplify the expression $g^2 - 6 + 6g^2 - 2 + h$.

   F $7gh^2 - 8$

   G $7g^2 - 8 + h$

   H $5g^2 - 8 + h$

   J $7g^2 - 8$

39. The cost for a group of people to visit the museum is given by the expression $8a + 5c$, where a is the number of adults and c is the number of children. What is the total cost for a group with 6 adults and 3 children?

A $33.00

B $63.00

C $72.00

D $78.00

40. Evaluate $8m^2 \div 3m$ for $m = 3$.

F 72

G 64

H 24

J 8

41. Evaluate $\frac{108}{x} \div 3y$ for $x = 2$ and $y = 3$.

A 6

B 12

C 18

D 27

42. To make a batch of fruit salad, Aaron needs 5 oranges and 7 apples. Oranges cost x and apples cost y. Write an expression equivalent to $15x + 21y$, which represents the cost of making 3 batches of fruit salad.

F $3(7x + 5y)$

G $3(5xy)$

H $3(5x + 7y)$

J $36xy$

43. Which is an example of the Distributive Property?

A $7(34) = 7(3) + 7(4)$

B $7 + (3 + 4) = (7 + 3) + 4$

C $7(34) = 7(30) + 7(4)$

D $7 + (3 + 4) = 7 + (4 + 3)$

44. $(18 + 13) + 7 = 18 + (13 + 7)$ is an example of which property?

F Commutative

G Associative

H Distributive

J Exponential

45. Which expression is equivalent to $6x + 3x^2 - 4x$?

A $3x^2 + 10x$

B $3x^2 - 2x$

C $2x - 3x^2$

D $2x + 3x^2$

46. Which two expressions are equivalent?

F $3x + 12$; $3(x + 3)$

G $2x + 24$; $2(x + 14)$

H $5x + 20$; $5(x + 6)$

J Not Here

47. Which expression is NOT equivalent to the expression $45 - 18$?

    A $3(15 - 6)$

    B 27

    C $(5 - 2)9$

    D $9(5 - 18)$

48. Margaret and Carl both purchased 2 jackets. Margaret spent $24.00 on one jacket and $32.00 on the other. Carl spent $28.00 on one jacket.

    $(\$24.00 + \$32.00); (\$28.00 + x)$

    What value of x makes the expressions equivalent?

    F $16.00

    G $24.00

    H $32.00

    J $28.00

49. Bobby and Veronica both have the same amount of money. Bobby has 4 one-dollar bills and 3 quarters. Veronica has only quarters. How many quarters does Veronica have?

    A 15 quarters

    B 17 quarters

    C 18 quarters

    D 19 quarters

50. Fareed and Mick are runners. On Wednesday, they started at the same point, but Fareed had a 30-minute head start. Fareed's pace is 35 yards per minute. Mick's pace is 45 yards per minute. The inequality $35(t + 30) < 45t$ represents the distance that each will run in t minutes when Mick is ahead of Fareed.

    At which of the following times would Mick be ahead of Fareed?

    F 60 minutes

    G 100 minutes

    H 110 minutes

    J Not Here

51. Which equation is true given $w = 7$?

    A $7w = 28$

    B $78 + w = 88$

    C $49 \div w = 7$

    D $83 - w = 7$

52. The inequality $g \leq 42$ represents the capacity of a standard bathtub. Which is a solution of the inequality?

    F $g = 42$

    G $g = 45$

    H $g = 52$

    J $g = 105$

53. Which value of x makes the equation true?

$$x - 9 = 12$$

A $x = 3$

B $x = 15$

C $x = 21$

D $x = 108$

54. To find out which colors are popular for cars, a parking lot was sampled. The results are shown in the table. If there are k fewer green cars than blue cars, write an algebraic expression for the number of green cars.

Color	Number of Cars
Black	38
Blue	19
Red	30
White	27
Other	32

F $k - 19$

G $k + 19$

H $19 - k$

J $19 + k$

55. Jasmine cut an apple into a equal slices. She ate 4 slices and had 4 slices left. Which equation models the situation?

A $a + 4 = 4$

B $4 - a = 2$

C $8a = 4$

D $a - 4 = 4$

56. A factory produces 150 whistles per hour. The number of hours at that rate is h. What is an expression for the number of whistles produced?

F $h + 150$

G $h - 150$

H $150h$

J $\dfrac{h}{150}$

57. What is an expression for the sequence in the table?

Position	1	2	3	4	5	n
Value of Term	4	7	10	13	16	

A $3n + 1$

B $3n - 1$

C $4n + 1$

D $4n - 1$

58. In a large fish tank, $\dfrac{1}{4}$ of the fish have black stripes on them. If 16 of the fish have black stripes, what is the total number of fish in the tank?

F 4

G 12

H 20

J 64

59. Lewis spent $12.27 on school supplies. He purchased notebooks and markers. The notebooks cost $7.93. Which equation can be used to find m, the cost of the markers?

A $m \div \$7.93 = \$12.27$

C $m + \$7.93 = \$12.27$

B $m \times \$7.93 = \$12.27$

D $m - \$7.93 = \$12.27$

---

60. Solve $5z = 105$.

F $z = 21$ **G** $z = 100$ **H** $z = 105$ **J** $z = 525$

---

61. Solve $p + 2\frac{4}{5} = 4\frac{1}{2}$.

A $p = 1\frac{3}{10}$ **B** $p = 1\frac{7}{10}$ **C** $p = 2\frac{3}{10}$ **D** $p = 2\frac{7}{10}$

---

62. Rajiv is building a bookcase. A shelf on the bookcase can hold up to 95 pounds of books. Which graph represents the situation?

F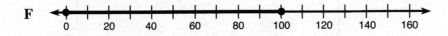

G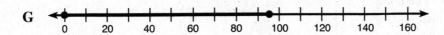

H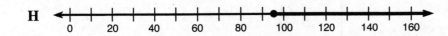

J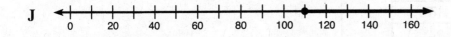

---

63. There are at least 27 visitors to the nurse's office each day at school. Which inequality represents the number of visitors to the nurse's office?

A $v < 27$ **B** $v > 27$ **C** $v \leq 27$ **D** $v \geq 27$

Expressions and Equations
Higher Scores on Math, Grade 6

64. Yesterday, more than 3 inches of rain fell. Which inequality represents this situation?

   F $y > 3$

   G $y < 3$

   H $y \leq 3$

   J $y \geq 3$

65. Which graph shows the solution to $y < -2.6$ on a number line?

   A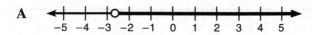

   B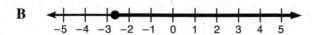

   C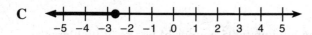

   D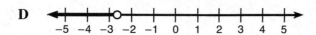

66. A rectangle has a length of 8 inches. The table shows the area of the rectangle for different widths. Write an expression that can be used to find the area of the rectangle when its width is w inches.

Length (in.)	Width (in.)	Area (in.²)
8	2	16
8	3	24
8	4	32
8	w	?

   F $w + 8$

   G $8w$

   H $\dfrac{8}{w}$

   J $32 + w$

67. Which ordered pair is a solution of the equation $y = 4x - 3$?

   A $(1, 3)$

   B $(3, 2)$

   C $(3, 1)$

   D $(2, 5)$

68. Which equation represents the graph of the line below?

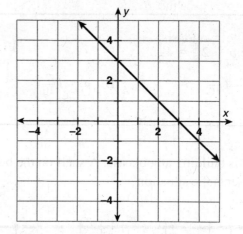

   F $y = 6x + 8$

   G $y = \dfrac{5}{7}x - 3$

   H $y = -x + 3$

   J $y = 2x - 1$

69. A parking garage charges $2.00 for the first hour and $0.50 for each fraction of an hour thereafter. Which statement describes the relationship between the parking fee and the amount of time a person parks in the garage?

A The parking fee depends on the amount of time a person uses the garage.

B The amount of time a person uses the garage depends on the parking fee.

C The parking fee and the amount of time a person uses the garage are independent.

D The relationship cannot be determined.

70. Tanya walks dogs. She earns $8.75 for each dog she walks. She wants to go to a concert that costs $70.00. Write an equation relating the number of dogs she needs to walk to the amount of money she wants to earn. Let n be the number of dogs Tanya walks.

F $\dfrac{8.75}{n} = 70$

G $8.75n = 70$

H $8.75 - n = 70$

J $8.75 + n = 70$

Geometry

Modeled Instruction

DIRECTIONS: Read each question and choose the best answer. Use the answer sheet provided at the end of the workbook to record your answers. If the correct answer is not available, mark the letter for "Not Here."

1. Find the area of the parallelogram.

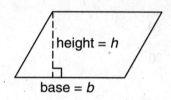

$h = 6$ cm, $b = 8$ cm

A 14 square centimeters

B 24 square centimeters

C 28 square centimeters

D 48 square centimeters

 Hint

If you decompose a parallelogram into two congruent right trapezoids and use them to compose a rectangle, the two figures have the same area. Thus you can use the formula $A = b \times h$ to find the area of a rectangle and a parallelogram.

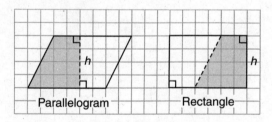

- The dashed line on the parallelogram is perpendicular to the base and divides the figure into two congruent pieces.

- If the shaded piece is moved to the right, the two pieces form a rectangle with *exactly* the same area.

Notice that the height of a parallelogram is *not* the length of one of its sides. It is the perpendicular distance from the base to the opposite side.

2. Find the area of the square.

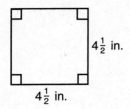

$4\frac{1}{2}$ in.

$4\frac{1}{2}$ in.

F 9 square inches

G 18 square inches

H $20\frac{1}{4}$ square inches

J $40\frac{1}{2}$ square inches

Hint

A square is a special type of rectangle with all sides equal. You can use the formula $A = bh$, or you can use this formula:
$A = s \times s$, or $A = s^2$.

3. Find the area of the right triangle.

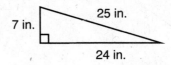

7 in.   25 in.

24 in.

A 42 square inches

B 56 square inches

C 84 square inches

D 168 square inches

Hint

The area of a right triangle is $\frac{1}{2}$ the area of a rectangle with the same base and height. On the rectangle below, a diagonal decomposes it into two congruent right triangles. Since the two triangles are congruent, the area of each triangle must be $\frac{1}{2}(b \times h)$. In right triangles, the height is the same as the length of one of the sides.

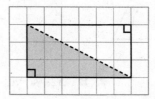

4. Find the area of the triangle.

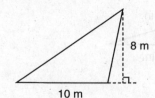

F 18 m²   **G** 36 m²   **H** 40 m²   **J** 80 m²

Hint

The *height* of a triangle is the perpendicular distance from the base to the vertex opposite the base. When the height is not a side of the triangle, a dashed line represents the height. For obtuse triangles, the height may be shown outside of the triangle. Extend the base just far enough to draw a perpendicular line to the opposite vertex. The length of the extended portion of the base is *not* used when calculating the area of the triangle.

---

5. Find the area of the trapezoid.

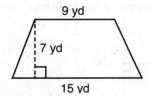

A $31\frac{1}{2}$ sq yd   **B** $52\frac{1}{2}$ sq yd   **C** 63 sq yd   **D** 84 sq yd

Hint

If you flip the trapezoid to the right, you compose a parallelogram made from 2 congruent trapezoids. Find the area of the parallelogram, and then divide by 2 to get the area of the trapezoid.

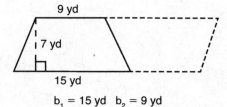

$b_1 = 15$ yd $b_2 = 9$ yd

6. Find the area of the regular polygon below.

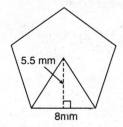

5.5 mm

8mm

F 200 mm²

G 110 mm²

H 67.5 mm²

J 40 mm²

Hint

A regular polygon has congruent sides and congruent angles. You can decompose any regular polygon into congruent triangles by drawing a line from the center of the polygon to each vertex. To find the area of the polygon, find the area of one of the triangles. Then multiply by the number of triangles formed.

7. The Nelsons will install new carpeting in their basement. Mr. Nelson made a drawing that shows the dimensions of the basement. Then he decomposed it into smaller figures.

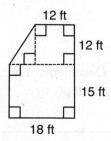

12 ft

12 ft

15 ft

18 ft

What is the area of the basement?

A 486 sq ft

B 450 sq ft

C 432 sq ft

D 414 sq ft

Hint

The dashed lines decompose the shape into two squares and a triangle. There are two ways to find the total area.

Method 1
• Find the area of the rectangle, the square, and the triangle formed by the dashed lines.

• Add the three areas to find the total area.

Method 2
• Extend the left side up and the top to the left to form an 18 by 27 rectangle.

• Find the area of this rectangle.

• Then subtract the area of the triangle formed that is not a part of the basement.

8. Rodney is making a game board in the shape of a regular hexagon. He divides the hexagon into congruent triangles, each with a base of 8 inches and a height of 7 inches. What is the area of the game board?

F 84 sq in.   **G** 90 sq in.   **H** 168 sq in.   **J** 336 sq in.

Hint

A hexagon has 6 sides. Decompose it into 6 congruent triangles. Then use the formula $A = \frac{1}{2}(bh)$ to find the area of one triangle and multiply by 6.

---

9. Devon finds the volume of a rectangular prism that is 3 units long, $1\frac{1}{2}$ units wide, and $1\frac{1}{2}$ units high by filling it with $\frac{1}{2}$-unit cubes.

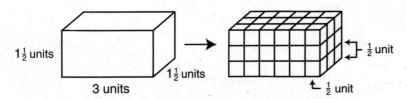

$1\frac{1}{2}$ units

3 units

$1\frac{1}{2}$ units

$\frac{1}{2}$ unit

$\frac{1}{2}$ unit

Then he removes the cubes and counts them. There are 54 cubes. What is the volume of the rectangular prism in cubic units?

A $6\frac{3}{4}$ cubic units   **B** $13\frac{1}{2}$ cubic units   **C** 54 cubic units   **D** 27 cubic units

Hint

It takes 8 half-unit cubes to make 1 unit cube.

Divide 54 by 8 to find the volume of the rectangular prism in cubic units.

$54 \div 8 = \square$

Use the volume formula to check your answer:

$V = lwh = 3 \times 1\frac{1}{2} \times 1\frac{1}{2} = \square$

Both methods should yield the same volume.

10. Find the volume of the rectangular prism.

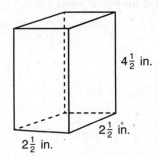

$4\frac{1}{2}$ in.

$2\frac{1}{2}$ in.

$2\frac{1}{2}$ in.

F $9\frac{1}{2}$ cubic inches

G $16\frac{1}{8}$ cubic inches

H $28\frac{1}{8}$ cubic inches

J $33\frac{1}{4}$ cubic inches

Hint

Substitute the given values into the formula for the volume of a rectangular prism. Rename each measure as an improper fraction. Then multiply. Remember, the Associative Property of Multiplication states that the grouping of the factors does not affect their product, so multiply in the order that is easiest for you.

11. Find the volume of a cube that measures 3.5 centimeters on each side.

A 10.5 cu cm

B 27.125 cu cm

C 31.5 cu cm

D 42.875 cu cm

Hint

The sides (*s*) of a cube are equal in length. Because the length, width, and height of a cube are the same, you use the formula:
A of a cube $= s^3$.

12. Find the volume of the composite solid figure.

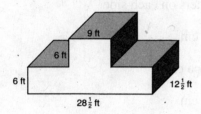

F 675 cu ft

G 1,350 cu ft

H $2,812\frac{1}{2}$ cu ft

J $4,218\frac{3}{4}$ cu ft

Hint

Decompose the figure into rectangular prisms. Find the volume of each prism. Then add to find the total volume. Here is one way to decompose the figure.

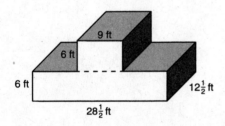

13. Casper will place point *F* to complete rectangle *EHMF*. Where should he place point *F*?

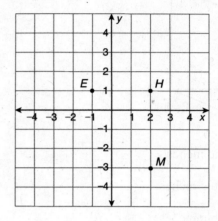

A (1, 3)

B (1, −3)

C (−1, −3)

D (−1, 3)

Hint

Side *EF* should be parallel to side *HM*. Point *F* will be directly below point *E*, and directly to the left of point *M*. This places it in Quadrant III. Use the signs for QIII.

For any point, if you know the quadrant in which a point is located, you also know the signs of its coordinates.

14. Anya draws points *E*, *H*, and *P* for isosceles trapezoid *EHMP*. She. Where should she place point *M*?

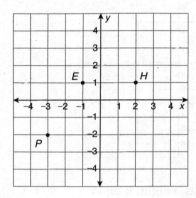

F (3, −2)

G (−3, −2)

H (4, −2)

J (−4, −2)

Hint

The location of point *M* must form a figure such that (1) side *PM* is parallel to side *EH*, and (2) side *HM* is the same length as side *EP*. One way to find the location of point *M* is to use logical reasoning: "I can get from point *E* to point *P*, if I move 2 units to the left and 3 units down. So I can get from point *H* to point *M* if I move 2 units to the right and 3 units down."

15. Felicia is drawing right triangle *PQR* on the graph below. Which could NOT be the location of point *P*?

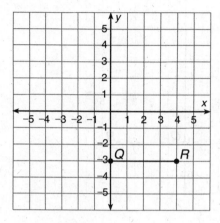

A (0, 0)

B (1, 4)

C (4, 0)

D (4, −5)

Hint

A right triangle has two sides that are perpendicular. Point *P* must have an *x*-coordinate that is the same as the *x*-coordinate for point Q or point *R*.

16. Suppose that Felicia placed point P at $(4, 5)$ on the graph below. What is the length of side RP?

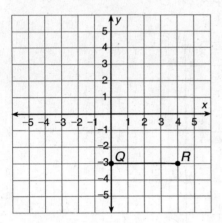

F 2 units

G 3 units

H 8 units

J 15 units

Hint

If P is at $(4, 5)$ and R is at $(4, -3)$, the two points are both 4 units to the right of the vertical axis (y-axis), and RP is a vertical line. To find the length of a *vertical line segment* using coordinates, add the y-coordinates. If the y-coordinates have different signs, add their absolute values.

$(4, 5)$ $|5| = 5$
$(4, -3)$ $|-3| = 3$
$5 + 3 = \square$, the length of RP

17. What are the dimensions of rectangle $WXYZ$?

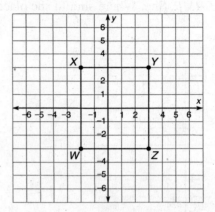

A base: 5 units, height: 6 units

B base: 4 units, height: 3 units

C base: 3 units, height: 4 units

D base 2 units, height: 6 units

Hint

The top and bottom sides are horizontal lines. To find the length of a *horizontal line segment* using coordinates, add the x-coordinates. If the x-coordinates have different signs, add their absolute values.

$W(-3, -2)$ $|-2| = 2$
$Z(3, -3)$ $|-3| = 3$
$2 + 3 = \square$, the length of side WZ

18. Reggie made this drawing of a corner flower garden for his yard. Then he mapped out the design on a coordinate plane. He placed the vertex for the right angle at (5, 2). What are the coordinates for the other vertices?

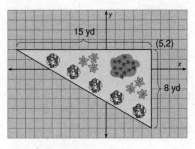

F (10, 2) and (5, 8)   **H** (15, −2) and (5, 6)

G (−10, 2) and (5, −6)   **J** (−15, 2) and (5, −8)

Hint

Use the given information: vertex at (5, 2), one leg = 15 yd, and one leg = 8 yd.
- Find the coordinates for a vertex that is 15 units directly to the left of (5, 2).
- Find the coordinates for a vertex that is 8 units directly below (5, 2).

---

19. Mariana folds the net below along the dashed lines. Which term best names the solid figure formed from the net?

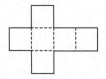

A rectangular prism   **B** triangular prism   **C** square pyramid   **D** cube

Hint

A net is a two-dimensional representation of a three-dimensional figure. All six parts of the net are squares, so the net forms a 6-sided solid with each face shaped like a square.

20. Which term names the solid figure formed from the net?

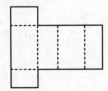

  F rectangular prism

  G square pyramid

  H square prism

  J Not Here

 Hint

The net is made from six rectangles with three different dimensions. Visualize what the solid figure will look like when the net is folded up. You may find it helpful to number or shade the areas that have the same dimensions. When the net is folded into a solid figure, these areas will be opposite sides.

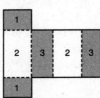

21. What solid figure can be made using this net?

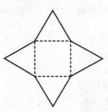

  A triangular pyramid

  B triangular prism

  C rectangular prism

  D square pyramid

 Hint

Make observations about the net. It is made up of 1 square and 4 triangles that appear to be congruent. Think: When folded, the net will form a solid figure with 1 square face that is the base and 4 triangular faces that appear to meet at a point.

22. Which net can Derek use to make a triangular prism?

F   G   H   J

 Hint

A triangular prism has exactly 2 congruent triangular faces and 3 rectangular faces. Identify any net that meets these conditions. Think: The triangular faces must be opposite of each other. Identify the net that, when folded, will meet this condition.

---

23. Demy needs to find the total surface area of a small box. She unfolds the box to make a net, as shown below.

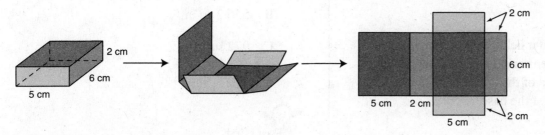

What is the surface area of the box?

A 46 cm²   **B** 52 cm²   **C** 92 cm²   **D** 104 cm²

 Hint

Surface area is the total area of the surface of a figure. Because the surfaces are flat, surface area is measured in square units. The box is a rectangular prism, so its opposite sides are congruent. Use the given information to find the dimensions of each surface. Then write and solve an equation to find the surface area.

Front/back faces: Top/bottom faces: Left/right faces:
5 cm × 2 cm   5 cm × 6 cm   6 cm × 2 cm

Name _____ Date _____

24. Find the surface area of the square pyramid below.

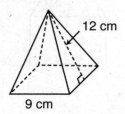

12 cm

9 cm

F 135 cm²

G 216 cm²

H 297 cm²

J 540 cm²

 Hint

You may find it helpful to draw a net and label its dimensions. Find the *lateral surface area*, the area of the 4 triangular faces. Then add the area of the base.

25. Martin makes lampshades from rice paper and wire coat hangers. For the design below, the lampshade is open at both ends. How much rice paper will he need if he makes 2 lampshades using the design and pattern below?

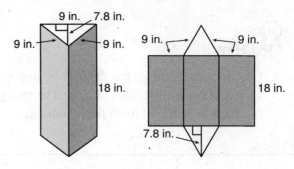

9 in.   7.8 in.

9 in.   9 in.

18 in.

9 in.   9 in.

18 in.

 7.8 in.

A 486 sq in.

B 556.2 sq in.

C 972 sq in.

D 1,112.4 sq in.

Hint

The information given says that the lampshade is open at the top and the bottom, and that Martin will make two lampshades. Consider these conditions when you calculate how much rice paper is needed.

Geometry

Independent Practice

DIRECTIONS: Read each question and choose the best answer. Use the answer sheet provided at the end of the workbook to record your answers. If the correct answer is not available, mark the letter for "Not Here."

26. Find the area of the parallelogram.

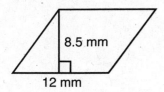

    F 41 mm²

    G 50 mm²

    H 51 mm²

    J 102 mm²

27. Find the area of the isosceles trapezoid.

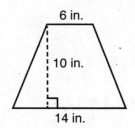

    A 40 in.²

    B 100 in.²

    C 420 in.²

    D 840 in.²

28. Find the area of a square with sides 28 cm.

    F 112 cm²

    G 392 cm²

    H 784 cm²

    J Not Here

29. The figure below is a regular polygon. What is its area?

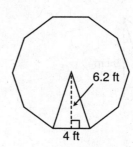

    A 81.6 ft²

    B 99.2 ft²

    C 102 ft²

    D 124 ft²

30. An area rug is shaped like a regular hexagon. The length of one side is 3 feet. The distance from the midpoint of the side to the center is 2.6 feet. What is the area of the rug?

    F 23.4 ft²

    G 31.2 ft²

    H 33.6 ft²

    J 44.8 ft²

31. Find the area of the triangle.

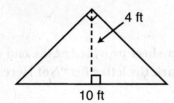

    A 20 ft²

    B 40 ft²

    C 80 ft²

    D 120 ft²

32. Nadine sketched an obtuse triangle with base 12 m and height 9 m. What is the area of the triangle?

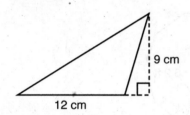

    F 29.25 cm²

    G 54 cm²

    H 67.5 cm²

    J 108 cm²

33. Kareem drew the triangle below. What is the area of the triangle?

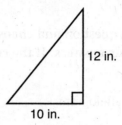

    A 22 in.²

    B 60 in.²

    C 70 in.²

    D 120 in.²

34. Perry has drawn this trapezoid. He writes three equations and says they all will give the correct area.

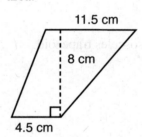

Equation A $A = \frac{1}{2}(11.5 + 4.5)8$

Equation B $A = \frac{1}{2}[(2 \times 11.5) + (2 \times 4.5)]8$

Equation C $A = (11.5 + 4.5)8 \div 2$

Is Perry correct?

    F Yes. All the equations will give the correct area.

    G No. Only equations A and B will give the correct area.

    H No. Only equations A and C will give the correct area.

    J No. Only equations B and C will give the correct area.

35. Yasuko decomposes this figure into smaller shapes to find its area.

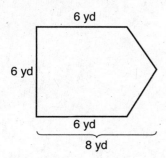

What is the area of the figure? (Hint: One way to decompose it is into a square and a triangle.)

A   26 yd²

B   39 yd²

C   42 yd²

D   48 yd²

36. Find the area of the shaded region of the figure.

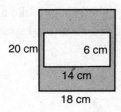

F   360 cm²

G   276 cm²

H   84 cm²

J   56 cm²

37. Andrea measured a shape in a quilt. Then she drew this sketch.

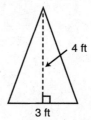

What is the area of the shape she measured?

A   6 square feet

B   7 square feet

C   12 square feet

D   14 square feet

38. A parallelogram has these measures:

base = 7.5 ft   height = 8.2 ft

What is the area of the parallelogram?

F   15.375 ft²

G   16.1 ft²

H   30.75 ft²

J   61.5 ft²

39. Find the area of a square with sides that measure 4.6 inches.

A   10.58 in.²

B   18.4 in.²

C   21.16 in.²

D   97.336 in.²

40. Find the area of the regular polygon.

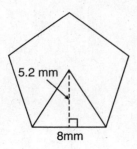

5.2 mm

8mm

F 104 mm²

G 135 mm²

H 166.4 mm²

J 332.8 mm²

41. A cube measures 25.5 cm on each side. What is the volume of the cube?

A 76.5 cm³

B 102 cm³

C 650.25 cm³

D Not Here

42. Tavia filled a container with $\frac{1}{2}$-inch cubes. She counted the cubes to find the volume. What is the volume of the container? (Hint: How many $\frac{1}{2}$-inch cubes = 1 cu in.?)

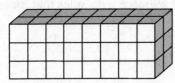

Each cube = $\frac{1}{2}$ cu in.

F 6 cu in.

G 8 cu in.

H 12 cu in.

J 24 cu in.

43. Malcolm fills a container with 72 cubes that are one-half cm each. What is the volume of the container?

A 8 cm³

B 9 cm³

C 12 cm³

D 18 cm³

44. A stack of newspapers in the recycling bin measures $8\frac{1}{2}$ inches long and 11 inches wide by 16 inches high. What is the volume of the stack of newspapers?

F $280\frac{1}{2}$ cu in.

G 748 cu in.

H 1,496 cu in.

J $1,542\frac{3}{4}$ cu in.

45. Mr. Burnet had a storage shed shaped like a rectangular prism. He added additional space to each side of the shed.

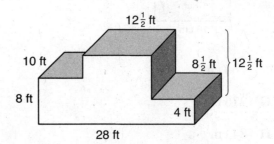

$12\frac{1}{2}$ ft

10 ft

$8\frac{1}{2}$ ft $12\frac{1}{2}$ ft

8 ft

4 ft

28 ft

What is the volume of his shed now?

A 876.25 cu ft

B $1,056\frac{1}{4}$ cu ft

C $2,462\frac{1}{2}$ cu ft

D 4,260 cu ft

46. Liam has a crate with the dimensions shown below. What is the volume of the box?

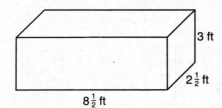

3 ft

2½ ft

8½ ft

F 14 cu ft

G 28 cu ft

H 42½ cu ft

J 63¾ cu ft

47. Yuan has some storage boxes like the one below. He uses some to make a 2-box by 2-box stack.

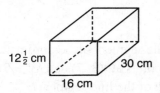

12½ cm

30 cm

16 cm

What is the volume of the stack?

A 48,000 cu cm

B 24,000 cu cm

C 12,000 cu cm

D Not Here

48. Roxanne bought this storage cube for her office.

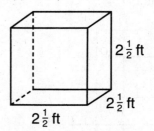

2½ ft

2½ ft

2½ ft

What is the volume of the storage cube?

F $7\frac{1}{2}$ cu ft

G $8\frac{1}{8}$ cu ft

H $15\frac{5}{8}$ cu ft

J $16\frac{1}{2}$ cu ft

49. Demaris will place point *A* to complete rectangle *ABCD*. Where should she place point *A*?

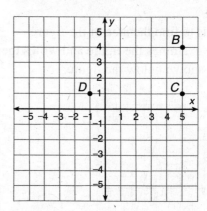

A (1, 4)

B (1, −4)

C (−1, 4)

D (−1, −4)

50. Michael is drawing parallelogram *ABCD*. Where should he place point *D*?

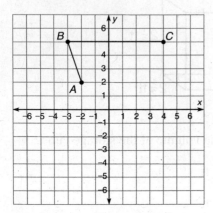

F (2, 5)

G (3, 2)

H (5, 2)

J (5, 3)

51. Susan needs to find the area of the figure below. She examines the figure and writes the statements shown below the figure.

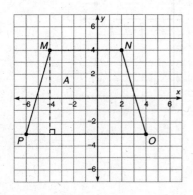

$(-6, -3)$ $|-6| = 6$
$(4, -3)$ $|4| = 4$
$6 + 4 = \square$, the length of side ___ .

Susan is calculating the length of which side?

A Side *MP*   **C** Side *MN*

B Side *NO*   **D** Side *PO*

52. Darla draws three vertices of a rectangle. Where should she place the fourth vertex?

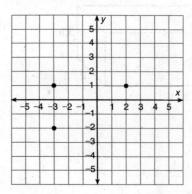

F (2, 2)

G (−2, −2)

H (2, −2)

J (−2, 2)

53. Joanne draws a line segment on a coordinate plane. It has end points at: (3, 7) and (3, −5). What is the length of the line segment?

A 4 units

B 9 units

C 12 units

D 25 units

54. Use the coordinates of the vertices to find the dimensions of rectangle *ABCD*.

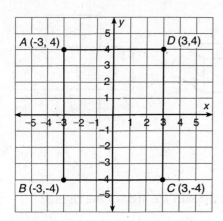

F length 3 units, width 4 units

G length 8 units, width 6 units

H length 9 units, width 12 units

J Not Here

55. If figure *WXYZ* is a right trapezoid, where should point *Z* be placed?

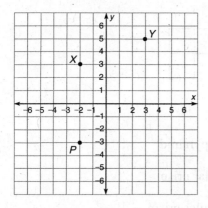

A (3, −1)

B (3, −3)

C (3, −5)

D Not Here

56. Tamara will draw right triangle *JKL*. First she draws line segment *JK*. Which could NOT be the location of point *L*?

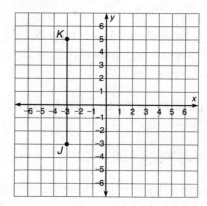

F (6, −3)

G (−5, 5)

H (4, −3)

J (−3, 3)

57. Three of the vertices of a square are: (−3, 2), (2, 2), and (2, −3). What are the coordinates of the fourth vertex?

A (3, −5)

B (−3, −3)

C (5, 5)

D (−5, −3)

58. Use the coordinates of rectangle *QRST* to find the length of side *QT*.

$Q\,(-3, 5)$ $R\,(5, 5)$
$T\,(-3, -2)$ $S\,(5, -2)$

Distance of *Q* from 0 on *y*-axis is $|5| = 5$.
Distance of *T* from 0 on *y*-axis is $|-2| = 2$.
The length of *QT* is 7 units.

Which statement about the length calculated is true?

F   It is correct. The length of *QT* is 7 units.

G It is incorrect. Use $|-3| = 3$ for the vertical distance of *T* from 0.

H It is incorrect. Subtract $5 - 2$ to find the vertical distance.

J   It is incorrect. This calculation is for a horizontal distance.

59. Which net will NOT form a cube when folded?

1 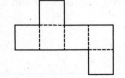   **3**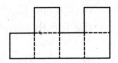

2 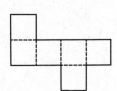   **4**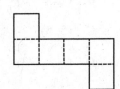

A Net 1

B Net 2

C Net 3

D Net 4

60. Dominic made a net to find the surface area of this rectangular prism.

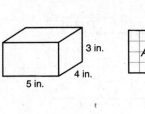 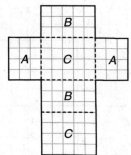

What is the surface area of the figure?

F   47 in.²

G 82 in.²

H 94 in.²

J   154 in.²

61. Leaette folds the net below along the dashed lines. Which term best names the solid figure formed from the net?

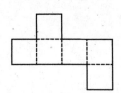

A cube

B square pyramid

C triangular prism

D rectangular prism

62. Sam folds the net below along the lines. What solid figure does he make?

   F   square pyramid

   G   rectangular pyramid

   H   rectangular prism

   J   triangular prism

63. Josie made a net for this triangular prism.

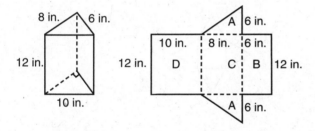

Use the net to find the surface area of the figure.

   A   312 in.²

   B   336 in.²

   C   360 in.²

   D   624 in.²

64. Use the net to find the surface area of the figure.

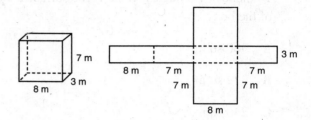

   F   134 m²   **H**   208 m²

   G   202 m²   **J**   282 m²

65. Tai builds sets for plays. She built a square pyramid with a base that measures 7.5 feet on each side. Its triangular faces have a height of 16 feet. Which expression can be used to find the surface area of the pyramid in square feet?

   A $7.5^2 + 4(0.5 \times 7.5 \times 16)$

   B $7.5^2 + (0.5 \times 7.5 \times 16)$

   C $7.5^2 \times 4(0.5 \times 7.5 \times 16)$

   D $7.5^2 \times (0.5 \times 7.5 \times 16)$

66. Walter folds the net below along the dashed lines. What solid figure does he make?

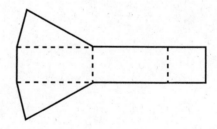

   F   triangular pyramid

   G   triangular prism

   H   rectangular pyramid

   J   rectangular prism

67. Eddie has a box that measures 6 inches by 10 inches by 6 inches. What is the surface area of the box?

   A 360 sq in.

   B 312 sq in.

   C 240 sq in.

   D 192 sq in.

68. Which net will form this solid figure?

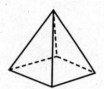

   F

   G

   H

   J

Statistics and Probability

Modeled Instruction

DIRECTIONS: Read each question and choose the best answer. Use the answer sheet provided at the end of the workbook to record your answer. If the correct answer is not available, mark the letter for "Not Here."

1. Which question is likely to show statistical variability in its answer?

   A How many seconds are equivalent to one minute?

   B What is the sum of 5 and 4?

   C How many months of the year begin with the letter *a*?

   D On what day of the week was a person born?

    Hint

   A statistical question is a question about a set of data that can vary. To answer a statistical question, you need to collect or look at a set of data. If the answer to a question will always be the same, it is not a statistical question.

2. A sales manager oversees the sale of cars at his car lot. Which of the following questions does NOT show variability in its answer?

   F How many cars does he sell each week?

   G How many customers does he talk to each week?

   H How many cars did he sell yesterday?

   J How many phone calls does he make each day?

    Hint

   Look for a question where the answer will not vary. For example, the number of cars he sells each week can change from week to week, so it is a statistical question.

3. What is a statistical question that could be asked about the data shown in this table?

Trail Lengths	
Trail	Length (miles)
Pinkney	1.75
Armstead	2.34
Oak	1.69

A How many people hiked each trail in one week?

B In what state is the shortest trail?

C How much longer is the Pinkney Trail than the Oak Trail?

D How many miles long is the Armstead Trail?

 Hint

Make up a possible answer for each question. Which answer will have variability?

4. Mr. Cruz used a dot plot to display the number of questions that each student answered correctly on the math quiz. Which statement describes the data?

Math Quiz

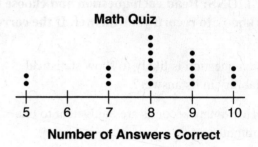

Number of Answers Correct

F There is a cluster from 5 to 7.

G The median of the data is 7.5.

H The mode of the data is 8.

J There is a gap at 7.

 Hint

Start by eliminating the answer choices that you know are not true. Since most of the data on the dot plot is 8 or greater, you know that the median cannot be less than 8.

Name _____ Date _____

Use this histogram to answer questions 5 and 6.

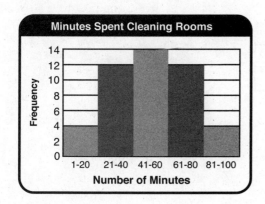

5. This histogram shows the number of minutes that sixth-graders spend cleaning their rooms each week. Which statement does NOT describe the data correctly?

A There are no gaps.

B There is one peak at interval 61–80.

C The graph has symmetry.

D Most students spend 60 minutes or less cleaning their rooms.

 Hint

You are looking for a statement that is incorrect as it relates to the data in the graph. Read each statement in the answer choices and compare it to the data in the graph. A graph has symmetry if you can fold it on the middle point and the data will match on each side of the line of symmetry.

6. In which interval would you find an estimate of the median?

F 1–20

G 21–40

H 41–60

J 81–100

 Hint

Decide if this graph has symmetry. If it does, then the median would appear at the center of the data distribution.

7. Which of the following is a measure of variation?

A mean

B median

C mode

D range

 Hint

You should know that a measure of center summarizes all of the values with a single number. A measure of variation describes how the values vary with a single number. You subtract the lowest number from the highest number to find the range.

Name _____ Date _____

Use this table of data to answer questions 8 and 9.

Prices of MP3 Players	
Electronic City	$24.00, $108.00, $30.00, $44.00, $62.00, $80.00
Best Electronics	$69.00, $42.00, $120.00, $59.00, $66.00, $76.00

8. What is the mean price of Best Electronics MP3 players?

F 58   **G** 65   **H** 72   **J** 80

Hint

You can find the mean of a set of data by adding all the values and dividing the sum by the number of values in the data set. Be sure to find the mean for Best Electronics.

9. The prices of MP3 players at Electronic City and Best Electronics are shown in the table. Which statement is true?

A The range of the prices at Electronic City is greater than the range of the prices at Best Electronics.

B The variation between the prices at each store is the same.

C The mean price at Electronic City is greater than the mean price at Best Electronics.

D The median price at Electronic City is greater than the median price at Best Electronics.

Hint

You need to compute the mean, median, and range for each store. Then compare the results to answer the question.

10. Paloma sells fruit and vegetables at the farmer's market. This dot plot shows the number of pounds she sells each day. What is the most common number of pounds that Paloma sells?

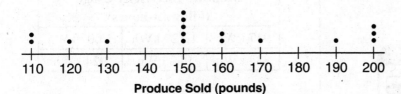

Produce Sold (pounds)

F 110 pounds   **G** 150 pounds   **H** 160 pounds   **J** 200 pounds

Hint

You are looking for the data point that appears most often. That means the number with the most dots over it. This number is called the mode.

---

11. The box plot displays data for the ages of students in dance class. What is the median of the data?

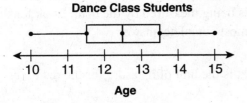

Dance Class Students

Age

A 10

B 15

C 12.5

D 13.5

Hint

On a box plot the median is the dot that is halfway between the lowest and highest values. Medians are not always whole numbers.

12. This histogram shows the monthly cell phone usage of customers with a family plan. Which group of minutes is used by the greatest number of customers?

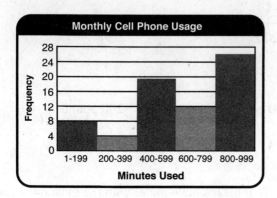

F   0–199

G   400–599

H   600–799

J   800–999

Hint

It makes sense that the highest bar represents the greatest number of customers.

Use this table of data to answer questions 13 and 14.

Monthly Electricity Usage (kilowatt-hours)		
917 kWh	1,129 kWh	1,007 kWh
837 kWh	983 kWh	924 kWh

13. The table shows data collected by an electricity supplier. What attribute is being measured?

A   monthly electricity usage

B   kilowatt-hours

C   electricity meter

D   time

Hint

The labels of tables can often tell you what is being measured by the data. Look for the most complete answer.

14. What is the unit of measure for the data set?

F   hours

G   inches

H   days

J   kilowatt-hours

Hint

An electricity meter measures electrical usage. What is the name of the unit of measure you usually see on your electric bill?

Use this table of data to answer questions 15 and 16.

Heights of Television Towers (meters)			
457	502	498	526
678	619	564	642

15. What attribute is being measured?

   A   number of towers

   B   heights of television towers

   C   number of televisions

   D   Not Here

   Hint

   Always look at the table label to decide what the data are describing.

16. How many observations are in the data set shown in this table?

   F   2

   G   4

   H   6

   J   8

   Hint

   Each number is an observation. The total number of values is the total number of observations.

17. Every day for one week, Keller recorded the number of customers who bought blueberry muffins at his cafe. The customer counts are 13, 8, 12, 15, 11, 20, and 19. What is the mean of the data?

   A   11

   B   12

   C   13

   D   14

   Hint

   Remember that to find the mean you add all the data values and divide by the number of data items. This will give you the mean number for the complete data set.

18. Todd and his friends collect coins. The numbers of coins in their collections are 45, 73, 86, 24, 57, 100, 58, 86, 68, and 74. What is the median of the data?

   F   67.1

   G   70.5

   H   76

   J   15

   Hint

   Remember that to find the median you must first write all the data values in consecutive order from least to greatest. Then you can mark off data values from each end of the list until you have one center value or two center values. If there are two center values, find the mean.

Name _____   Date _____

19. Michelle recorded the number of customers who bought plain bagels at her bakery each day for one week. The customer counts are 15, 7, 6, 9, 10, 12, and 11. What is the range of the data?

A 6

B 9

C 10

D 15

 Hint

Remember that to find the range of a set of data, you must subtract the least (smallest) data value from the greatest data value. The difference is the range of the data.

20. The dot plot shows the number of history books borrowed from the library each day during a 10-day period. The mean of the number of books borrowed each day is 8. What is the mean absolute deviation?

History Books Borrowed

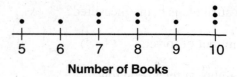

Number of Books

F 14

G 10

H 1.5

J 1.4

 Hint

The mean absolute deviation tells how far away the data values are from the mean.

First: Make a list of all the distances and how far away they are from the mean.

Second: Find the mean of the distances by finding the sum of the distances and dividing by 10 because there are 10 data values. The quotient is the mean absolute deviation.

Statistics and Probability
Higher Scores on Math, Grade 6

Use this box plot to answer questions 21 and 22.

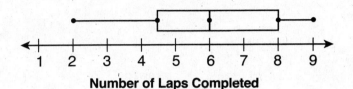

Number of Laps Completed

21. The box plot shows the number of laps completed on a track. What are the lower and upper quartiles?

A   4.5, 8

B   4.5, 6

C   6, 8

D   2, 9

Hint

The median of the data is 6. The lower quartile is the median of the lower half of the data. The upper quartile is the median of the upper half of the data.

22. What is the interquartile range?

F   1.5

G   2

H   3.5

J   Not Here

Hint

A measure of variability is a single number that describes how far apart the numbers are in a data set. Interquartile range is a measure of variability. To find the interquartile range, subtract the lower quartile from the upper quartile.

23. The prices of karaoke machines at 6 different stores are $77.00, $85.00, $78.00, $72.00, $80.00, and $245.00. What is the outlier in the data set?

A $74.00

B $79.00

C $85.00

D $245.00

Hint

Sometimes a data set contains a number that is much less or much greater than the rest. This number is called an outlier.

24. The amounts of money Gillian earned each week from babysitting are $5.00, $10.00, $20.00, $10.00, $15.00, $5.00, $42.00, and $5.00. How is the mean of the data set affected when the outlier is removed?

F   The mean is unchanged.

G   The mean increases by $4.00.

H   The mean decreases by $4.00.

J   The mean increases by $1.00.

Hint

Outliers can affect the mean. Find the mean with and without the outlier to see how it changes.

25. Vishal compared the prices of a video game at several different stores. The prices are $43.00, $64.00, $38.00, $36.00, $37.00, $34.00, and $28.00. Which measure of center best describes the prices?

A median

B mode

C mean

D range

Hint

Notice that most prices are in or near the thirties. Remember that outliers affect the mean rather than the median.

Statistics and Probability

Independent Practice

DIRECTIONS: Read each question and choose the best answer. Use the answer sheet provided at the end of the workbook to record your answers. If the correct answer is not available, mark the letter for "Not Here."

26. What is a statistical question that could be answered from the data shown in the table?

Age of Schools	
School Name	**Age**
Canyon Creek Elementary	12 years
Johnson Elementary	3 years
Lewis Middle School	10 years
Armstrong High School	8 years

F   What is the average age of schools in the school district?

G   How many students attend the middle school?

H   How many classrooms are there in the elementary school building?

J   How many daily class periods are there in the high school?

27. Explain why the question "How many colors are there in the United States flag?" is NOT a statistical question.

A   There are a limited number of possible answers.

B   The answer may change over time.

C   The variability in the data is limited.

D   There is no variability in the data.

28. Under what condition is "How many hours per week do you work?" a statistical question?

F   The question is asked of a job applicant.

G   The question is asked of the president of a company.

H   The question is asked of all employees of a company.

J   The question is asked of a person who does not work for the company.

29. The heights of the students in your class are being recorded. Which question is a statistical question for this situation?

A   What is the average height of students in your class?

B   Is Tranh taller than Sylvia?

C   How tall is Patrick?

D   How many students are in your class?

30. The line plot shows the number of medals won by the 15 sixth-grade classes that participated in a mini-Olympics. Where do most of the scores cluster?

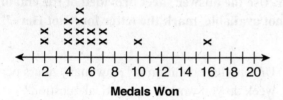

Medals Won

F around 10

G at the higher end of the range

H around 15

J at the lower end of the range

31. The data set and box plot show the times, in minutes, for 16 restaurant orders.

Describe the shape of the data distribution.

7, 9, 11, 13, 13, 15, 12, 17, 18, 13, 9, 7, 12, 16, 18, 10

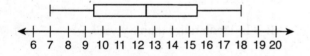

A The data distribution is skewed to the right. The mean is much greater than the median.

B The data distribution is approximately symmetric. The mean and median are nearly equal.

C The data distribution is skewed to the left. The mean is much less than the median.

D There is not enough information to tell whether or not the data distribution is skewed.

32. The manager of an amusement park takes a survey to find out the ages of the people who ride a new ride. The results of the survey are shown in the histogram. Around what value(s) do the data cluster?

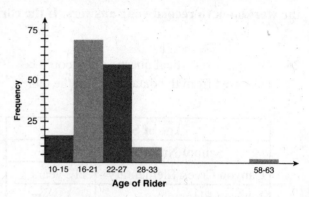

Age of Rider

F The data cluster around the values 10–21.

G The data cluster around the values 16–27.

H The data cluster around the values 22–33.

J Not Here

33. Luisa is making a histogram for the following set of data: 11, 77, 35, 5, 76, 34, 89, 92, 22. Which is an appropriate first interval if she plans to use 10 intervals?

A 0−5

B 0−10

C 0−50

D 0−100

34. The weights of five trout caught in Lake Placid are 3 lb, 1 lb 1 oz, 2 lb 15 oz, 2 lb 9 oz, and 1 lb 1 oz. What is the median weight of the five fish?

F 2 lb 12 oz

G 2 lb 15 oz

H 2 lb 9 oz

J 1 lb 1 oz

35. Cindy struck out 7, 14, 6, 4, 5, and 6 batters in softball games this season. In discussing her stats with a newspaper reporter, Cindy's coach mentions that the average number of Cindy's strikeouts is 7. Is the coach's statement misleading?

    A No; the mean of her strikeouts is 7.

    B Yes; she struck out 7 batters only one time.

    C Yes; the median of her strikeouts is 7.

    D No; she typically strikes out 7 batters in a game.

---

36. The number of calls responded to by a paramedic team over an 8-day period are given. Which box-and-whisker plot correctly shows the data?

12, 6, 8, 15, 14, 6, 14, 10

  F 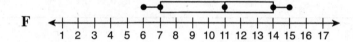

  G 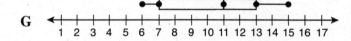

  H 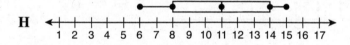

  J 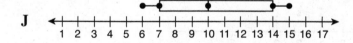

---

37. Which data set does the line plot represent?

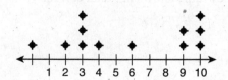

  A 0, 2, 2, 3, 3, 4, 6, 9, 9, 9, 10, 10

  B 0, 2, 3, 3, 3, 3, 4, 9, 9, 10, 10, 10

  C 0, 2, 3, 3, 3, 4, 6, 9, 9, 10, 10, 10

  D 0, 2, 3, 3, 4, 4, 5, 6, 9, 9, 10, 10

38. Which data set could the histogram represent?

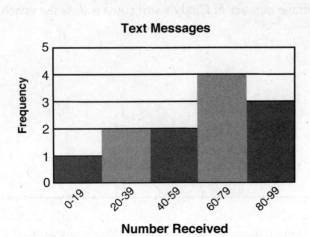

F 6, 12, 33, 45, 59, 68, 70, 76, 79, 82, 94, 96

G 6, 21, 33, 45, 59, 68, 70, 76, 83, 85, 94, 96

H 6, 21, 33, 39, 59, 68, 70, 76, 79, 82, 94, 96

J 6, 21, 33, 45, 59, 68, 70, 76, 79, 82, 94, 96

39. Kendra asked her friends how many pets they each had in their family. Which plot matches Kendra's data?

4, 2, 1, 1, 0, 2, 7, 3, 1, 0, 0

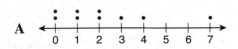

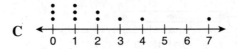

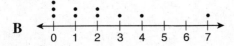

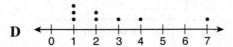

40. Sarita recorded the number of minutes the bus was late. Which frequency table shows her data correctly organized?

3, 7, 0, 4, 10, 6, 8, 5, 3, 11, 12, 0, 7, 4, 8, 17, 15, 12, 13, 5

F

Minutes late	0–5	5–10	10–15	15–20
Frequency	8	8	5	2

H

Minutes late	0–5	5–10	10–15	15–20
Frequency	8	6	5	1

G

Minutes late	0–5	6–10	11–15	16–20
Frequency	8	6	5	1

J

Minutes late	0--5	6–10	11–15	16–20
Frequency	5	4	4	1

41. Doug counts the number of boys and girls in his math class and makes a frequency table. How many students are in his class?

Student	Boy	Girl
Frequency	12	13

A 12

B 13

C 25

D 26

42. Your friend asks a group of sixth graders how many DVDs they purchased within the past two years. Your friend shows you a dot plot he made to represent the data. How many sixth graders did he ask?

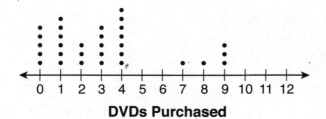

DVDs Purchased

F 8

G 9

H 27

J 31

43. Dr. Furh measures the length and mass of a hamster. Which units is she most likely to use?

A millimeters, grams

B millimeters, kilograms

C meters, grams

D meters, kilograms

44. Lucas read an article about his town. The article gave the following data: 1912; 1,075 ft; 62°F; 4,007. In order, what do the data describe about his town?

F elevation, temperature, population, date founded

G date founded, elevation, temperature, population

H population, elevation, temperature, date founded

J date founded, population, temperature, elevation

45. Dr. McDermott measured four dogs and recorded the data in the table shown.

Dog	Measurement
Gracie	16.5 kg
Pebbles	5.5 kg
Bailey	29.6 kg
Emmit	14.1 kg

What attribute did Dr. McDermott measure?

A temperature

B mass

C height

D length

46. What is the median of the following group of numbers?

111   110   120   118   115   113

F 114.83

G 114

H 115

J 118

47. Find the interquartile range of this data set.

7, 13, 9, 15, 11, 7, 11

A 13

B 11

C 7

D 6

48. Find the median of the data set.

15, 9, 19, 13, 23, 22, 11

F 11

G 14

H 15

J 16

49. The table shows the number of stories in eight buildings. Which statement about the data is true?

Number of Stories							
15	15	18	20	22	24	26	60

A The mode is greater than the mean.

B There are no outliers.

C The mode best describes the data.

D The mean is greater than the median.

50. The dot plot shows the number of playoff games played by fifteen members of the Boston Bruins ice hockey team during the playoffs for the 2010-2011 season. Which statement about the data is true?

Games Played, 2010-2011 Playoffs

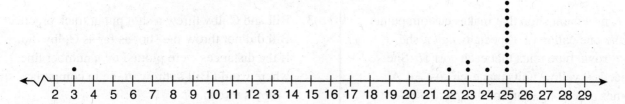

F   The outlier makes the mean less than it would otherwise be.

H   The outlier makes the mean greater than it would otherwise be.

G   The outlier makes the median less than it would otherwise be.

J   The outlier makes the median greater than it would otherwise be.

Practice Test A

DIRECTIONS: Read each question and choose the best answer. Use the answer sheet provided at the end of the workbook to record your answers. If the correct answer is not available, mark the letter for "Not Here."

1. Sara owns a paint shop that makes custom paints. To make one gallon of a specialty color, she needs 4 royal blue units that each cost b. She also needs 9 yellow units that each cost y. A customer orders 4 gallons of this paint.

   Sara uses the expression $4(4b + 9y)$ to find the total cost for the color units needed to make each gallon of paint. Which is another way to write this expression?

   A 144by

   B $16b + 9y$

   C $4(13by)$

   D $16b + 36y$

2. Nikki sold 25 tickets to the school play and Lakisha sold 47 tickets. What is the ratio of the number of tickets Nikki sold to the number of tickets Lakisha sold?

   F 47 to 25

   G 25 to 47

   H 25 to 72

   J 47 to 72

3. Bill and Colby threw a shot put at track practice. Bill did not throw the shot as far as Colby did. If the distances were plotted on a number line, where would Bill's throw, B, be in comparison to Colby's throw, C?

   A B would be to the left of C, but to the right of 0.

   B B would be to the right of C.

   C B and C would be at the same location.

   D B and C would both be to the left of 0.

4. Calvin made a wooden frame that he will cover with canvas, as shown below. What is the area of the frame?

   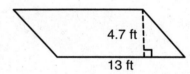

   F 17.7 ft²

   G 30.66 ft²

   H 35.4 ft²

   J 61.1 ft²

5. Which question is a statistical question?

   A How many students are on the basketball team?

   B How many students are in Mrs. Johnson's math class?

   C How old are you?

   D How old is a typical student in the school?

6. The table shows scores on a math quiz. Which statement about the data is true?

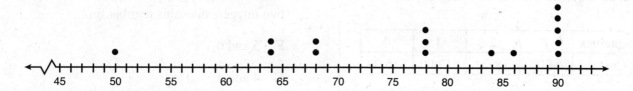

F The data cluster around the median.

G The mode is the best measure of center to describe the data.

H The data value 50 is not an outlier.

J Not Here

---

7. Henry's parents give him an allowance every week. They use the expression $\frac{1}{2}a + 2$, in which a is Henry's age, to calculate how much allowance he gets, in dollars. What is Henry's allowance when he is 10 years old?

A $5.00   **B** $7.00   **C** $10.00   **D** $22.00

---

8. What are the coordinates of point B?

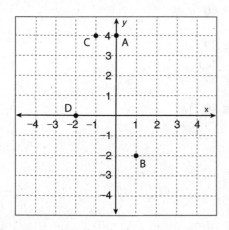

F $(-1, 2)$ **G** $(1, -2)$ **H** $(-1, -2)$ **J** $(1, 2)$

9. The table shows the price of different numbers of magazines. Predict the cost of 5 magazines.

Magazines	1	2	3	4
Cost	$4.00	$8.00	$12.00	$16.00

A $14.00

B $20.00

C $22.00

D $24.00

10. Divide. Express your answer in simplest form.

$4\frac{1}{2} \div 1\frac{1}{4}$

F $3\frac{3}{5}$

G $5\frac{5}{8}$

H 5

J $4\frac{1}{2}$

11. Jim needs to buy x T-shirts for his club. He was quoted a price of $5.00 per shirt plus a $40.00 set up fee. Which expression gives the total cost of the T-shirts?

A $5(x + 40)$

B $5 + 40x$

C $5x + 40$

D Not Here

12. The integer 4.65 represents the amount of tax Nicholas had to pay on a bill. Between which two integers does this number lie?

F 5 and 6

G 4 and 5

H −4 and 4

J −4 and −5

13. The Gresner family paid $385.00 for 5 nights at a hotel. What is the unit rate?

A $\frac{\$77.00}{1 \text{ night}}$

B $\frac{\$154.00}{1 \text{ night}}$

C $\frac{\$385.00}{1 \text{ night}}$

D $\frac{\$39.00}{1 \text{ night}}$

14. There are at least 89 visitors to the botanical gardens each day. Which inequality represents the number of visitors to the botanical gardens?

F $v < 89$

G $v \geq 89$

H $v > 89$

J $v \leq 89$

15. Devora finds the volume of a rectangular prism that is 3 units long, $1\frac{1}{2}$ units wide, and $2\frac{1}{2}$ units high by filling it with $\frac{1}{2}$-unit cubes.

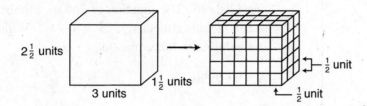

She removes the cubes and counts them. There are 90 cubes. What is the volume of the rectangular prism in cubic units?

A 90 cubic units   **B** $78\frac{3}{4}$ cubic units   **C** $11\frac{1}{4}$ cubic units   **D** 9 cubic units

---

16. The table shows the number of minutes that Mary spent working on her math homework each day this week.

Monday	Tuesday	Wednesday	Thursday	Friday
47	42	45	46	10

Which value is the LEAST accurate description of the center of Mary's data set? Why?

F The mean of the data set; the outlier 10 will cause the mean to be less than most of the data values.

G The median of the data set; the outlier 10 will cause the median to be less than most of the data values.

H The mean of the data values for Monday, Tuesday, Wednesday, and Thursday; this mean will describe only four of the data values.

J The median of the data values for Monday, Tuesday, Wednesday, and Thursday; this median will describe only four of the data values.

---

17. Which figure will be formed when the net is folded on the dashed lines?

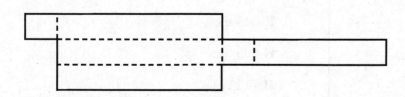

A rectangular pyramid   **B** rectangular prism   **C** triangular prism   **D** square pyramid

18. For the equation represented by the graph below, what is the value of y when x is -1?

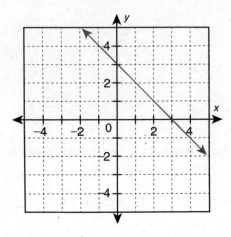

F 0

G 4

H 6

J -10

19. Louise needs r colored pencils in addition to the 10 pencils she already has. Which expression shows the number of pencils Louise needs?

A $10 \div r$

B $10 - r$

C $10 + r$

D $10r$

20. Gloria is selling orange juice before the beginning of a morning swim meet. If she has 18 pints of juice, how many 1-cup servings can she sell?

F 9 cups

G 36 cups

H 72 cups

J 144 cups

21. Wendy and Jacinda are comparing their sea shell collections. Over the past year, Wendy collected 4 more than 2 times as many as Jacinda. Wendy has 42 shells. The equation to find the number of shells Jacinda collected is $2s + 4 = 42$. Which is a solution to this equation?

A 80 shells

B 76 shells

C 23 shells

D 19 shells

22. Luanda wants to buy a box of cereal. Which box has the lowest cost per ounce?

F 20-oz box for $3.20

G 16-oz box for $2.72

H 15-oz box for $2.25

J 10-oz box for $1.70

23. Brigitta's car will hold 26 cartons of books. What is the least number of trips that she must make in order to deliver 250 cartons?

A 5 trips

B 10 trips

C 15 trips

D 20 trips

24. Sammy needs 5^3 tiles to complete his mosaic. How many tiles does he need?

F 15 tiles

G 25 tiles

H 125 tiles

J 625 tiles

25. The number of T-shirts sold at Brent's T-shirts and T-shirt City during the last 6 days are shown in the table.

T-shirts Sold	
Brent's T-shirts	24, 80, 30, 108, 44, 62
T-shirt City	69, 42, 76, 59, 66, 120

Which statement is true?

A The variation between the number of T-shirts sold is the same.

B The mean number of T-shirts sold at Brent's T-shirts is greater than the mean number of T-shirts sold at T-shirt City.

C The interquartile range of the number of T-shirts sold at Brent's T-shirts is greater than the interquartile range of the number of T-shirts sold at T-shirt City.

D The median number of T-shirts sold at Brent's T-shirts is greater than the median number of T-shirts sold at T-shirt City.

26. Rob has a rectangular garden space at a community garden. He places stakes at three of the corners of the garden, as shown on the map. Where should be place the stake for the fourth corner?

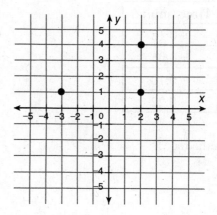

F (3, 4)

G (3, −4)

H (−3, 4)

J (−3, −4)

27. What is an expression for the missing value in the table?

Dogs	1	2	3	n
Legs	4	8	12	

A 4

B $n + 3$

C $4n$

D $n + 1$

28. In a car race, Elvin's car finished in third place with a time of 56 minutes and 14 seconds. The table shows the times of the other racers as compared to Elvin's time.

Racer	Time (min:s)
Annie	+0:18
John	−0:06
Roy	−0:10
Emily	+0:22

Who won the race?

F Emily

G John

H Roy

J Annie

29. Frank's Sports store has a 20% off sale on all of its merchandise. How much is the discount on a baseball glove that originally costs $25.00?

A $0.05

B $5.00

C $20.00

D $30.00

30. A piece of wood measuring 42 inches was cut into equal pieces. If each piece was 2.8 inches long, how many pieces were cut?

F 10 pieces

G 12 pieces

H 14 pieces

J 15 pieces

31. Sally runs 7.2 miles every day. How far does she run in 5 days?

A 12.2 miles

B 36 miles

C 43.2 miles

D 50.4 miles

32. In which quadrant is the point $(-3, 5)$?

F Quadrant I

G Quadrant II

H Quadrant III

J Quadrant IV

33. Which expression contains a product, a sum, and a quotient?

A $\dfrac{3x(7 + 3)}{4}$

B $3x - 3$

C $\dfrac{1}{2(8x - 4)}$

D $4x^2 + 11x - 3$

34. José uses **this** net to find the surface area of a rectangular **prism**.

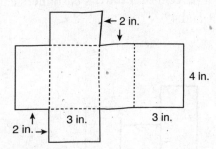

What is the surface area of the prism?

F 24 in.^{2}

G 26 in.^{2}

H 48 in.^{2}

J 52 in.^{2}

35. Mrs. Samuelson records the amount of time each of her students spends studying each week. Which line plot correctly shows the data?

Number of Hours
1 2 4 3 2 1 2 3 3 2 1 1 1 2 1

A

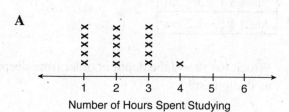

B

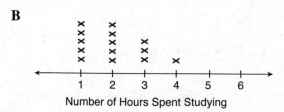

C

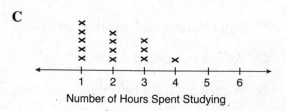

D

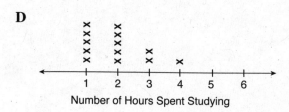

36. David recorded the depth at which he planted 4 different seeds.

Seed	Depth
Seed 1	−2.5 cm
Seed 2	−4.6 cm
Seed 3	−5.9 cm
Seed 4	−1.2 cm

Which list shows the depth in order from deepest to shallowest?

F   −5.9, −4.6, −1.2, −2.5

G   −5.9, −4.6, −2.5, −1.2

H   −1.2, −2.5, −4.6, −5.9

J   −2.5, −1.2, −5.9, −4.6

37. Which situation could be represented by the integer +7?

A   A dog is 7 years old.

B   A student misses 7 questions on a quiz.

C   An oak tree loses 7 acorns.

D   A child has lost 7 baby teeth.

38. The histogram shows the number of customers at Yvette's Pets at different times of day during one week. What percent of Yvette's customers came between 11 and 4?

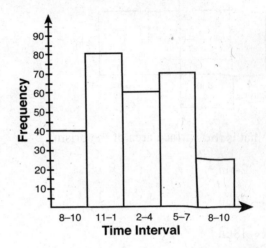

F   about 70%

G   about 51%

H   about 65%

J   about 29%

39. Use the map to answer the question.

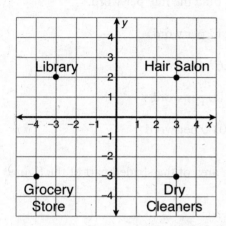

Cesar leaves the hair salon and goes to the library. How many blocks west does he walk?

A   6 blocks

B   5 blocks

C   3 blocks

D   2 blocks

40. Selena draws one side of a triangle *EFG*, as shown. If the triangle is an acute triangle, which could be the location of vertex *G*?

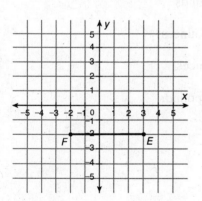

F $(-2, 3)$

G $(-4, 2)$

H $(3, 1)$

J $(1, 5)$

41. Which of the following has value that is less than 0?

A $|8|$

B $-|8|$

C 8

D $|-8|$

42. Ivonne collected the following data about her parents' car: 12.7 gallons, 2,452 pounds, 132 miles per hour, 14.6 feet. In order, which attributes of the car do the data describe?

F   fuel tank volume, length, top speed, weight

G   weight, top speed, length, fuel tank volume

H   length, weight, fuel tank volume, top speed

J   fuel tank volume, weight, top speed, length

43. Renee works at the Candy Boutique making gift candy arrangements. Each arrangement must have the same number of truffles and the same number of hard candies. If she has 16 truffles and 24 hard candies, and uses all of the pieces of candy, what is the greatest number of arrangements she can make?

A   2 arrangements

B   3 arrangements

C   6 arrangements

D   8 arrangements

44. Find a set of 5 items that has a range of 9, a mean of 15, a median of 14, and a mode of 11.

F   11, 11, 13, 15, 20

G   5, 11, 14, 14, 31

H   11, 11, 14, 19, 20

J   6, 10, 14, 15, 15

45. Hun is calculating the length of one side of trapezoid *ABCD*. His work is shown below.

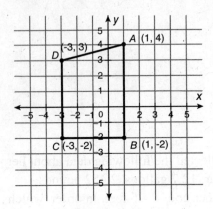

$(-3, -2) |{-2}| = 2 \qquad (-3, 3) |3| = 3$

Hun is calculating the length of which side?

A Side *CD*

B Side *DA*

C Side *AB*

D Side *BC*

46. King Sea Cruise Lines booked 1,256 passengers for a trip to the Bahamas. There were 164 cancellations. How many people took the cruise?

F 1,092 people

G 1,044 people

H 1,468 people

J 1,821 people

47. What is $8 \times 8 \times 8 \times 8$ written in exponential form?

A 32

B 8^4

C 4,096

D 4^8

48. A writer was paid $12,000.00 for a 2,000-word article. Find the rate per word.

F $0.17 per word

G $1.67 per word

H $6.00 per word

J $60.00 per word

49. Find the area of the shaded part of the figure.

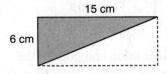

A 21 cm²

B 42 cm²

C 45 cm²

D 90 cm²

50. Dr. Katz measured the length and weight of a frog. Which units is he most likely to use?

F feet, pounds

G inches, ounces

H feet, ounces

J inches, pounds

Practice Test B

DIRECTIONS: Read each question and choose the best answer. Use the answer sheet provided at the end of the workbook to record your answers. If the correct answer is not available, mark the letter for "Not Here."

1. Which frequency table correctly organizes the data?

   1.3, 0.1, 1.1, 34.6, 5.9, 8.3, 12.5, 1.0, 0.7, 0.8, 28.2, 16.7, 0.2, 5.2

   A

Length	<0.5	0.5–5	5–10	>10
Frequency	4	3	3	4

   C

Length	0–9	10–19	20–29	30–39
Frequency	9	3	1	1

   B

Length	<0.5	0.5–5	5–10	>10
Frequency	2	5	4	3

   D

Length	0–9	10–19	20–29	30–39
Frequency	10	2	1	1

2. Write the ratio as a fraction in simplest form.

   20:45

   F $\dfrac{9}{13}$ **G** $\dfrac{13}{9}$ **H** $\dfrac{4}{9}$ **J** $\dfrac{9}{4}$

3. Ori is a personal trainer. He lifts weights for $\frac{1}{2}$ hour before each of his sessions. If he had 3 sessions last week, how many hours did he lift weights last week?

   A $\frac{1}{3}$ hour   **B** $\frac{3}{4}$ hour   **C** $1\frac{1}{2}$ hours   **D** 6 hours

4. Fernando bought a box of candy with x pieces. He ate 12 of them. Which expression represents the number of pieces left in the box?

   F $x + 12$ **G** $x - 12$ **H** $x \div 12$ **J** $12x$

5. A boat is decorated with triangular canvas flags for a Fourth of July celebration. The diagram below shows the dimensions of the flags.

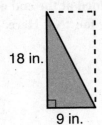

18 in.

9 in.

What is the area of the shaded triangle?

A 40.5 in.²   **B** 81 in.²   **C** 121.5 in.²   **D** 162 in.²

---

6. The box-and-whisker plots show the lifespans, in days, of two different brands of light bulbs. Which set of statements correctly describes how the data distributions are alike and how they are different?

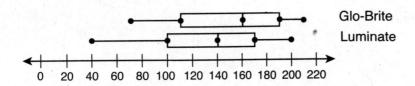

Glo-Brite

Luminate

0 20 40 60 80 100 120 140 160 180 200 220

F Both data sets appear to be right-skewed.

The center of the Glo-Brite data is greater than the center of the Luminate data.

The spread of the Luminate data is greater than the spread of the Glo-Brite data.

G Both data sets appear to be symmetrically distributed.

The center of the Luminate data is greater than the center of the Glo-Brite data.

The spread of the Glo-Brite data is greater than the spread of the Luminate data.

H Both data sets appear to be symmetrically distributed.

The center of the Luminate data is greater than the center of the Glo-Brite data.

The spread of the Luminate data is greater than the spread of the Glo-Brite data.

J Both data sets appear to be right-skewed.

The center of the Glo-Brite data is greater than the center of the Luminate data.

The spread of the Glo-Brite data is greater than the spread of the Luminate data.

Name _____ **Date** _____

7. In which equation does $n = 8$?

   A $n + 25 = 18$ **B** $7 = 56n$ **C** $7.8 - n = 0.2$ **D** $\frac{7}{8}n = 7$

---

8. Solve for g in the following equation: $\frac{8g}{11} = 4$.

   F $g = 3\frac{3}{11}$ **G** $g = 2\frac{10}{11}$ **H** $g = 5\frac{1}{2}$ **J** $g = 4\frac{8}{11}$

---

9. Find the day in which Allana accomplished the most tasks per hour.

Day	Number of Tasks	Hours
Monday	5	8
Tuesday	10	4
Wednesday	8	5
Thursday	5	5
Friday	7	7

   A Monday   **B** Tuesday   **C** Thursday   **D** Friday

---

10. Solve the equation. Choose the answer in simplest form.

    $4x = \frac{8}{7}$

    F $\frac{1}{28}$ **G** $\frac{1}{7}$ **H** $\frac{2}{7}$ **J** $\frac{7}{2}$

---

11. Use the number line to compare points A and D.

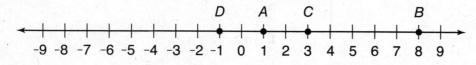

    A $D > A$ **B** $A < D$ **C** $A > D$ **D** Not Here

12. A fish tank has a base that measures 32.5 in. and a width that measures 18.3 in. Its height is 12 in. If the tank is filled to the top, how many cubic inches of water will it hold?

F   7,137 cubic inches of water

G   615.6 cubic inches of water

H   606.75 cubic inches of water

J   195 cubic inches of water

13. While doing a report on weather records for your town, you write a statistical question about daily temperature records for one year. Which of the statements below could NOT be the answer to your question?

A   August had the highest average daily temperature.

B   The highest temperature during January was 52°F.

C   The average low temperature for September was 48°F.

D   The range of temperatures from March 1 to May 1 was 50°F.

14. Use the data in the table to write an equation.

x	y
−2	−2
2	10
4	16

F $y = 2x - 1$

G $y = 3x + 4$

H $y = 6x - 2$

J $y = 5x + 3$

15. Star draws a line segment on a coordinate plane. It has endpoints $(-6, 5)$ and $(2, 5)$. What is the length of the line segment?

A   11 units

B   10 units

C   8 units

D   4 units

16. The table shows the number of points Gina and Tori scored during soccer practice last week.

Number of Points	
Gina	5, 3, 1, 6, 0, 2, 4
Tori	6, 5, 4, 6, 3, 7, 4

Which statement is true?

F   The range of Gina's points is the same as the range of Tori's points.

G   The mean of Gina's points is greater than the mean of Tori's points.

H   The mean of Gina's points is the same as the mean of Tori's points.

J   The number of Gina's points varied more from game to game than the number of Tori's points.

17. Which expression is equal to "the quotient of a number and 8"?

A $n \div 8$

B $n \times 8$

C $n - 8$

D $n + 8$

18. On a map of a college campus, the computer science building is located at (3, 2). The dining hall is located 5 units south of the computer science building. What ordered pair represents the location of the dining hall?

F (−2, 2)   **G** (3, −3)   **H** (8, 2)   **J** (8, 7)

---

19. The table shows prices per pound. Which graph shows the same data?

Pounds	1	2	3	4
Price ($)	3	6	9	12

A
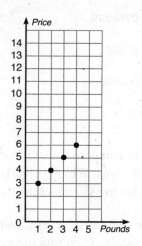

C
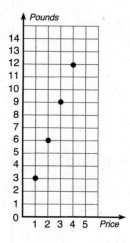

B
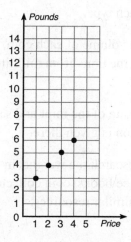

D
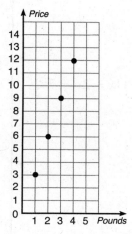

---

20. Find the quotient of 2,488 ÷ 12.

F $27\frac{1}{3}$ **G** $207\frac{1}{3}$ **H** 2,476   **J** 2,500

21. Simplify the expression $2 \times 4^2 - 8 \div 4$.

    A   30

    B   24

    C   6

    D   4

22. A waffle recipe uses 3 cups of mix for 4 waffles. How much mix would you need to make 12 waffles?

    F   12 c

    G   9 c

    H   8 c

    J   6 c

23. What is the least common multiple of 3 and 8?

    A   2

    B   3

    C   24

    D   48

24. Which expression is equivalent to $11x + 2x^3 - 7x$?

    F $2x^3 + 4x$

    G $4x - 2x^3$

    H $18x - 2x^3$

    J $2x^3 - 4x$

25. Which figure will be formed when the net is folded on the dashed lines?

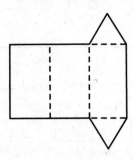

    A   rectangular pyramid

    B   rectangular prism

    C   triangular pyramid

    D   triangular prism

26. Maureen wants to compare the weights of different types of coins. Which is NOT a reasonable way for her to collect the data?

    F   Measure the weights of several coins of each type using a scale. Then find the average weight for each type.

    G   Calculate the volume of each coin. Then change the units from milliliters to milligrams.

    H   Visit the website of the mint and see whether the information is given there.

    J   Attempt to research the weights in a library, using reference books, coin collectors' manuals, or similar resources.

27. Write the inequality shown by the graph.

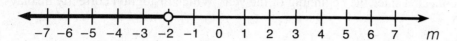

A $m \leq -2$

B $m \geq -2$

C $m < -2$

D $m > -2$

28. The average temperature in Cottonville in September is 72°F. The temperature was below average for 4 days last week by the amount indicated in the chart.

Day	Below Average
Monday	$-1.2°$
Wednesday	$-2°$
Thursday	$-0.7°$
Friday	$-0.45°$

Which list shows the days in order from warmest to coldest?

F Wednesday, Monday, Thursday, Friday

G Monday, Wednesday, Thursday, Friday

H Thursday, Friday, Wednesday, Monday

J Friday, Thursday, Monday, Wednesday

29. Each day, a golf course surveys golfers to find out the number of golf balls that were lost on the course. The frequency table shows the data collected since the beginning of the year. Which histogram correctly displays the data?

Number of Golf Balls Lost	Frequency
0–49	44
50–99	32
100–149	29
150 or more	35

A
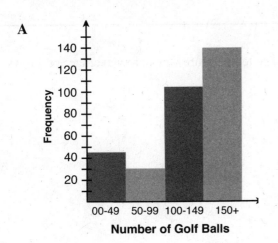

C
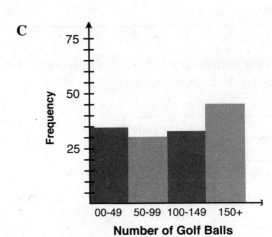

B
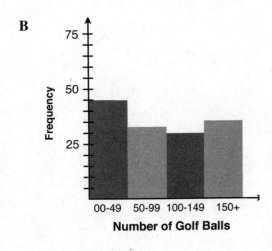

D
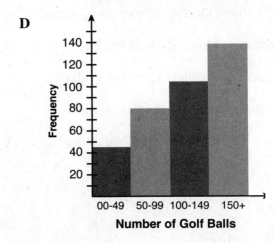

30. Which number added to −1 gives the sum of 0?

F −1 **G** 1 **H** −2 **J** 0

31. Coach Patel is buying food for the end-of-season celebration for his baseball team. He wants to buy 9 pizzas that cost $\$p$ each and 27 chicken wings that cost $\$w$ each. If each pizza costs $11.00 and the chicken wings are $1.05 apiece, what is the total cost?

- **A** $354.15
- **B** $306.45
- **C** $127.35
- **D** $108.45

32. Which number represents being paid $34.50?

- **F** −34.50
- **G** −3450
- **H** +34.50
- **J** +3.450

33. What is 35% of 220?

- **A** .77
- **B** 7.7
- **C** 770
- **D** Not Here

34. Find the mean and median of the data set.

35, 40, 37, 36, 42, 42, 34

- **F** mean: 38; median: 37
- **G** mean: 38; median: 42
- **H** mean: 37; median: 38
- **J** mean: 42; median: 37

35. Livia filled a container with $\frac{1}{2}$-unit cubes. She counted the cubes to find the volume. What is the volume of the container?

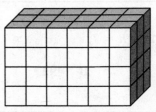

Each cube = $\frac{1}{8}$ cu unit

- **A** 9 cubic units
- **B** 13 cubic units
- **C** 64 cubic units
- **D** 72 cubic units

36. In the expression $6x^2 + 3x - 3$, $6x^2$, $3x$, and 3 are examples of which of the following?

- **F** coefficients
- **G** variables
- **H** factors
- **J** terms

37. In which quadrant does the point (11, 1) lie?

- **A** Quadrant I
- **B** Quadrant II
- **C** Quadrant III
- **D** Quadrant IV

38. How many feet are there in 7 miles?

    F 3,696 ft   **G** 5,280 ft   **H** 7,040 ft   **J** 36,960 ft

---

39. Evaluate $68h + 4$ for $h = 7$.

    A 480   **B** 492   **C** 624   **D** 748

---

40. Start at the origin. Point J is 3 units right and 4 units down. What are the coordinates of J?

    F $(3, 4)$ **G** $(-3, 4)$ **H** $(3, -4)$ **J** $(-3, -4)$

---

41. Arletta and Keenan each plan to spend at least 20 minutes per day working out. The dot plots show the number of minutes per day each worked out for the first few weeks.

Which of the statements about the two data sets is true?

Arletta:

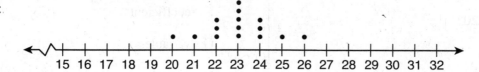

Keenan:

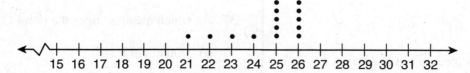

    A The data sets have the same median.   **C** The data sets have the same interquartile range.

    B The data sets both have outliers.   **D** The data sets have the same mode.

---

42. Find the absolute value of $|-47|$.

    F -47 **G** 0   **H** 1   **J** 47

43. A mountain biker completes a 35-mile track in 2.5 hours. What is the mountain biker's speed?

    A 12 miles per hour   **B** 14 miles per hour   **C** 35 miles per hour   **D** 87.5 miles per hour

---

44. A fish is swimming at a depth of 12 feet. A scuba diver is closer to the surface. Which describes the depth of the scuba diver?

    F depth of greater than -12 feet   **H** depth of less than 12 feet

    G depth of greater than 12 feet   **J** depth of less than -12 feet

---

45. Which shows four equivalent expressions for $6x + 8x$?

A		**B**		**C**		**D**	
1)	$3(2x) + 4(2x)$	1)	$3(2x) + 4(2x)$	1)	$2(3x) + 2(4x)$	1)	$6(x) + 8(x)$
2)	$(3 + 4)(2x + 2x)$	2)	$(3 + 4)2x$	2)	$(2 + 2)7x$	2)	$(6 + 8)(x \times x)$
3)	$7(4x)$	3)	$7(2x)$	3)	$4(7x)$	3)	$14(x^2)$
4)	$28x$	4)	$14x$	4)	$28x$	4)	$14x^2$

---

46. Find the area of the regular polygon.

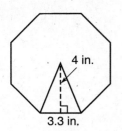

4 in.

3.3 in.

    F 26.4 in.^{2} **G** 52.8 in.^{2} **H** 79.2 in.^{2} **J** 105.6 in.^{2}

---

47. The line plot shows the number of books 12 students read in Ms. Zuber's book club during the summer. Which measure of central tendency best describes the data?

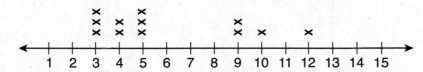

    A The mean is 6.   **B** The median is 5.   **C** The modes are 3 and 5.   **D** The range is 9.

48. Mr. Lin bought 5 new pairs of socks. He paid $21.25 for the five pairs. How much does one pair of socks cost?

F $4.01

G $4.25

H $5.23

J $106.25

49. Find the surface area of the rectangular prism. (Hint: Sketch a net if it is helpful.)

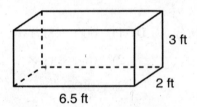

3 ft

2 ft

6.5 ft

A 34.5 ft²

B 37.2 ft²

C 64 ft²

D 77 ft²

50. If *d* represents how many dozens of eggs were ordered, which expression represents the number of eggs that were ordered?

F 12*d*

G 12 + *d*

H 12 ÷ *d*

J *d* ÷ 12

Answer Sheets

Pretest

1 Ⓐ Ⓑ Ⓒ Ⓓ	10 Ⓕ Ⓖ Ⓗ Ⓙ	19 Ⓐ Ⓑ Ⓒ Ⓓ	28 Ⓕ Ⓖ Ⓗ Ⓙ	37 Ⓐ Ⓑ Ⓒ Ⓓ	46 Ⓕ Ⓖ Ⓗ Ⓙ
2 Ⓕ Ⓖ Ⓗ Ⓙ	11 Ⓐ Ⓑ Ⓒ Ⓓ	20 Ⓕ Ⓖ Ⓗ Ⓙ	29 Ⓐ Ⓑ Ⓒ Ⓓ	38 Ⓕ Ⓖ Ⓗ Ⓙ	47 Ⓐ Ⓑ Ⓒ Ⓓ
3 Ⓐ Ⓑ Ⓒ Ⓓ	12 Ⓕ Ⓖ Ⓗ Ⓙ	21 Ⓐ Ⓑ Ⓒ Ⓓ	30 Ⓕ Ⓖ Ⓗ Ⓙ	39 Ⓐ Ⓑ Ⓒ Ⓓ	48 Ⓕ Ⓖ Ⓗ Ⓙ
4 Ⓕ Ⓖ Ⓗ Ⓙ	13 Ⓐ Ⓑ Ⓒ Ⓓ	22 Ⓕ Ⓖ Ⓗ Ⓙ	31 Ⓐ Ⓑ Ⓒ Ⓓ	40 Ⓕ Ⓖ Ⓗ Ⓙ	49 Ⓐ Ⓑ Ⓒ Ⓓ
5 Ⓐ Ⓑ Ⓒ Ⓓ	14 Ⓕ Ⓖ Ⓗ Ⓙ	23 Ⓐ Ⓑ Ⓒ Ⓓ	32 Ⓕ Ⓖ Ⓗ Ⓙ	41 Ⓐ Ⓑ Ⓒ Ⓓ	50 Ⓕ Ⓖ Ⓗ Ⓙ
6 Ⓕ Ⓖ Ⓗ Ⓙ	15 Ⓐ Ⓑ Ⓒ Ⓓ	24 Ⓕ Ⓖ Ⓗ Ⓙ	33 Ⓐ Ⓑ Ⓒ Ⓓ	42 Ⓕ Ⓖ Ⓗ Ⓙ	
7 Ⓐ Ⓑ Ⓒ Ⓓ	16 Ⓕ Ⓖ Ⓗ Ⓙ	25 Ⓐ Ⓑ Ⓒ Ⓓ	34 Ⓕ Ⓖ Ⓗ Ⓙ	43 Ⓐ Ⓑ Ⓒ Ⓓ	
8 Ⓕ Ⓖ Ⓗ Ⓙ	17 Ⓐ Ⓑ Ⓒ Ⓓ	26 Ⓕ Ⓖ Ⓗ Ⓙ	35 Ⓐ Ⓑ Ⓒ Ⓓ	44 Ⓕ Ⓖ Ⓗ Ⓙ	
9 Ⓐ Ⓑ Ⓒ Ⓓ	18 Ⓕ Ⓖ Ⓗ Ⓙ	27 Ⓐ Ⓑ Ⓒ Ⓓ	36 Ⓕ Ⓖ Ⓗ Ⓙ	45 Ⓐ Ⓑ Ⓒ Ⓓ	

Ratio and Proportion Modeled Instruction

1 Ⓐ Ⓑ Ⓒ Ⓓ	6 Ⓕ Ⓖ Ⓗ Ⓙ	11 Ⓐ Ⓑ Ⓒ Ⓓ	16 Ⓕ Ⓖ Ⓗ Ⓙ	21 Ⓐ Ⓑ Ⓒ Ⓓ
2 Ⓕ Ⓖ Ⓗ Ⓙ	7 Ⓐ Ⓑ Ⓒ Ⓓ	12 Ⓕ Ⓖ Ⓗ Ⓙ	17 Ⓐ Ⓑ Ⓒ Ⓓ	22 Ⓕ Ⓖ Ⓗ Ⓙ
3 Ⓐ Ⓑ Ⓒ Ⓓ	8 Ⓕ Ⓖ Ⓗ Ⓙ	13 Ⓐ Ⓑ Ⓒ Ⓓ	18 Ⓕ Ⓖ Ⓗ Ⓙ	23 Ⓐ Ⓑ Ⓒ Ⓓ
4 Ⓕ Ⓖ Ⓗ Ⓙ	9 Ⓐ Ⓑ Ⓒ Ⓓ	14 Ⓕ Ⓖ Ⓗ Ⓙ	19 Ⓐ Ⓑ Ⓒ Ⓓ	24 Ⓕ Ⓖ Ⓗ Ⓙ
5 Ⓐ Ⓑ Ⓒ Ⓓ	10 Ⓕ Ⓖ Ⓗ Ⓙ	15 Ⓐ Ⓑ Ⓒ Ⓓ	20 Ⓕ Ⓖ Ⓗ Ⓙ	25 Ⓐ Ⓑ Ⓒ Ⓓ

Ratio and Proportion Independent Practice

26 Ⓕ Ⓖ Ⓗ Ⓙ	32 Ⓕ Ⓖ Ⓗ Ⓙ	38 Ⓕ Ⓖ Ⓗ Ⓙ	44 Ⓕ Ⓖ Ⓗ Ⓙ	50 Ⓕ Ⓖ Ⓗ Ⓙ	56 Ⓕ Ⓖ Ⓗ Ⓙ
27 Ⓐ Ⓑ Ⓒ Ⓓ	33 Ⓐ Ⓑ Ⓒ Ⓓ	39 Ⓐ Ⓑ Ⓒ Ⓓ	45 Ⓐ Ⓑ Ⓒ Ⓓ	51 Ⓐ Ⓑ Ⓒ Ⓓ	57 Ⓐ Ⓑ Ⓒ Ⓓ
28 Ⓕ Ⓖ Ⓗ Ⓙ	34 Ⓕ Ⓖ Ⓗ Ⓙ	40 Ⓕ Ⓖ Ⓗ Ⓙ	46 Ⓕ Ⓖ Ⓗ Ⓙ	52 Ⓕ Ⓖ Ⓗ Ⓙ	58 Ⓕ Ⓖ Ⓗ Ⓙ
29 Ⓐ Ⓑ Ⓒ Ⓓ	35 Ⓐ Ⓑ Ⓒ Ⓓ	41 Ⓐ Ⓑ Ⓒ Ⓓ	47 Ⓐ Ⓑ Ⓒ Ⓓ	53 Ⓐ Ⓑ Ⓒ Ⓓ	59 Ⓐ Ⓑ Ⓒ Ⓓ
30 Ⓕ Ⓖ Ⓗ Ⓙ	36 Ⓕ Ⓖ Ⓗ Ⓙ	42 Ⓕ Ⓖ Ⓗ Ⓙ	48 Ⓕ Ⓖ Ⓗ Ⓙ	54 Ⓕ Ⓖ Ⓗ Ⓙ	60 Ⓕ Ⓖ Ⓗ Ⓙ
31 Ⓐ Ⓑ Ⓒ Ⓓ	37 Ⓐ Ⓑ Ⓒ Ⓓ	43 Ⓐ Ⓑ Ⓒ Ⓓ	49 Ⓐ Ⓑ Ⓒ Ⓓ	55 Ⓐ Ⓑ Ⓒ Ⓓ	

Number Sense Modeled Instruction

1 Ⓐ Ⓑ Ⓒ Ⓓ	6 Ⓕ Ⓖ Ⓗ Ⓙ	11 Ⓐ Ⓑ Ⓒ Ⓓ	16 Ⓕ Ⓖ Ⓗ Ⓙ	21 Ⓐ Ⓑ Ⓒ Ⓓ
2 Ⓕ Ⓖ Ⓗ Ⓙ	7 Ⓐ Ⓑ Ⓒ Ⓓ	12 Ⓕ Ⓖ Ⓗ Ⓙ	17 Ⓐ Ⓑ Ⓒ Ⓓ	22 Ⓕ Ⓖ Ⓗ Ⓙ
3 Ⓐ Ⓑ Ⓒ Ⓓ	8 Ⓕ Ⓖ Ⓗ Ⓙ	13 Ⓐ Ⓑ Ⓒ Ⓓ	18 Ⓕ Ⓖ Ⓗ Ⓙ	23 Ⓐ Ⓑ Ⓒ Ⓓ
4 Ⓕ Ⓖ Ⓗ Ⓙ	9 Ⓐ Ⓑ Ⓒ Ⓓ	14 Ⓕ Ⓖ Ⓗ Ⓙ	19 Ⓐ Ⓑ Ⓒ Ⓓ	24 Ⓕ Ⓖ Ⓗ Ⓙ
5 Ⓐ Ⓑ Ⓒ Ⓓ	10 Ⓕ Ⓖ Ⓗ Ⓙ	15 Ⓐ Ⓑ Ⓒ Ⓓ	20 Ⓕ Ⓖ Ⓗ Ⓙ	25 Ⓐ Ⓑ Ⓒ Ⓓ

Answer Sheets
Higher Scores on Math, Grade 6

Number Sense Independent Practice

26 Ⓕ Ⓖ Ⓗ Ⓙ	35 Ⓐ Ⓑ Ⓒ Ⓓ	44 Ⓕ Ⓖ Ⓗ Ⓙ	53 Ⓐ Ⓑ Ⓒ Ⓓ	62 Ⓕ Ⓖ Ⓗ Ⓙ	71 Ⓐ Ⓑ Ⓒ Ⓓ
27 Ⓐ Ⓑ Ⓒ Ⓓ	36 Ⓕ Ⓖ Ⓗ Ⓙ	45 Ⓐ Ⓑ Ⓒ Ⓓ	54 Ⓕ Ⓖ Ⓗ Ⓙ	63 Ⓐ Ⓑ Ⓒ Ⓓ	72 Ⓕ Ⓖ Ⓗ Ⓙ
28 Ⓕ Ⓖ Ⓗ Ⓙ	37 Ⓐ Ⓑ Ⓒ Ⓓ	46 Ⓕ Ⓖ Ⓗ Ⓙ	55 Ⓐ Ⓑ Ⓒ Ⓓ	64 Ⓕ Ⓖ Ⓗ Ⓙ	
29 Ⓐ Ⓑ Ⓒ Ⓓ	38 Ⓕ Ⓖ Ⓗ Ⓙ	47 Ⓐ Ⓑ Ⓒ Ⓓ	56 Ⓕ Ⓖ Ⓗ Ⓙ	65 Ⓐ Ⓑ Ⓒ Ⓓ	
30 Ⓕ Ⓖ Ⓗ Ⓙ	39 Ⓐ Ⓑ Ⓒ Ⓓ	48 Ⓕ Ⓖ Ⓗ Ⓙ	57 Ⓐ Ⓑ Ⓒ Ⓓ	66 Ⓕ Ⓖ Ⓗ Ⓙ	
31 Ⓐ Ⓑ Ⓒ Ⓓ	40 Ⓕ Ⓖ Ⓗ Ⓙ	49 Ⓐ Ⓑ Ⓒ Ⓓ	58 Ⓕ Ⓖ Ⓗ Ⓙ	67 Ⓐ Ⓑ Ⓒ Ⓓ	
32 Ⓕ Ⓖ Ⓗ Ⓙ	41 Ⓐ Ⓑ Ⓒ Ⓓ	50 Ⓕ Ⓖ Ⓗ Ⓙ	59 Ⓐ Ⓑ Ⓒ Ⓓ	68 Ⓕ Ⓖ Ⓗ Ⓙ	
33 Ⓐ Ⓑ Ⓒ Ⓓ	42 Ⓕ Ⓖ Ⓗ Ⓙ	51 Ⓐ Ⓑ Ⓒ Ⓓ	60 Ⓕ Ⓖ Ⓗ Ⓙ	69 Ⓐ Ⓑ Ⓒ Ⓓ	
34 Ⓕ Ⓖ Ⓗ Ⓙ	43 Ⓐ Ⓑ Ⓒ Ⓓ	52 Ⓕ Ⓖ Ⓗ Ⓙ	61 Ⓐ Ⓑ Ⓒ Ⓓ	70 Ⓕ Ⓖ Ⓗ Ⓙ	

Expressions and Equations Modeled Instruction

1 Ⓐ Ⓑ Ⓒ Ⓓ	6 Ⓕ Ⓖ Ⓗ Ⓙ	11 Ⓐ Ⓑ Ⓒ Ⓓ	16 Ⓕ Ⓖ Ⓗ Ⓙ	21 Ⓐ Ⓑ Ⓒ Ⓓ
2 Ⓕ Ⓖ Ⓗ Ⓙ	7 Ⓐ Ⓑ Ⓒ Ⓓ	12 Ⓕ Ⓖ Ⓗ Ⓙ	17 Ⓐ Ⓑ Ⓒ Ⓓ	22 Ⓕ Ⓖ Ⓗ Ⓙ
3 Ⓐ Ⓑ Ⓒ Ⓓ	8 Ⓕ Ⓖ Ⓗ Ⓙ	13 Ⓐ Ⓑ Ⓒ Ⓓ	18 Ⓕ Ⓖ Ⓗ Ⓙ	23 Ⓐ Ⓑ Ⓒ Ⓓ
4 Ⓕ Ⓖ Ⓗ Ⓙ	9 Ⓐ Ⓑ Ⓒ Ⓓ	14 Ⓕ Ⓖ Ⓗ Ⓙ	19 Ⓐ Ⓑ Ⓒ Ⓓ	24 Ⓕ Ⓖ Ⓗ Ⓙ
5 Ⓐ Ⓑ Ⓒ Ⓓ	10 Ⓕ Ⓖ Ⓗ Ⓙ	15 Ⓐ Ⓑ Ⓒ Ⓓ	20 Ⓕ Ⓖ Ⓗ Ⓙ	25 Ⓐ Ⓑ Ⓒ Ⓓ

Expressions and Equations Independent Practice

26 Ⓕ Ⓖ Ⓗ Ⓙ	34 Ⓕ Ⓖ Ⓗ Ⓙ	42 Ⓕ Ⓖ Ⓗ Ⓙ	50 Ⓕ Ⓖ Ⓗ Ⓙ	58 Ⓕ Ⓖ Ⓗ Ⓙ	66 Ⓕ Ⓖ Ⓗ Ⓙ
27 Ⓐ Ⓑ Ⓒ Ⓓ	35 Ⓐ Ⓑ Ⓒ Ⓓ	43 Ⓐ Ⓑ Ⓒ Ⓓ	51 Ⓐ Ⓑ Ⓒ Ⓓ	59 Ⓐ Ⓑ Ⓒ Ⓓ	67 Ⓐ Ⓑ Ⓒ Ⓓ
28 Ⓕ Ⓖ Ⓗ Ⓙ	36 Ⓕ Ⓖ Ⓗ Ⓙ	44 Ⓕ Ⓖ Ⓗ Ⓙ	52 Ⓕ Ⓖ Ⓗ Ⓙ	60 Ⓕ Ⓖ Ⓗ Ⓙ	68 Ⓕ Ⓖ Ⓗ Ⓙ
29 Ⓐ Ⓑ Ⓒ Ⓓ	37 Ⓐ Ⓑ Ⓒ Ⓓ	45 Ⓐ Ⓑ Ⓒ Ⓓ	53 Ⓐ Ⓑ Ⓒ Ⓓ	61 Ⓐ Ⓑ Ⓒ Ⓓ	69 Ⓐ Ⓑ Ⓒ Ⓓ
30 Ⓕ Ⓖ Ⓗ Ⓙ	38 Ⓕ Ⓖ Ⓗ Ⓙ	46 Ⓕ Ⓖ Ⓗ Ⓙ	54 Ⓕ Ⓖ Ⓗ Ⓙ	62 Ⓕ Ⓖ Ⓗ Ⓙ	70 Ⓕ Ⓖ Ⓗ Ⓙ
31 Ⓐ Ⓑ Ⓒ Ⓓ	39 Ⓐ Ⓑ Ⓒ Ⓓ	47 Ⓐ Ⓑ Ⓒ Ⓓ	55 Ⓐ Ⓑ Ⓒ Ⓓ	63 Ⓐ Ⓑ Ⓒ Ⓓ	
32 Ⓕ Ⓖ Ⓗ Ⓙ	40 Ⓕ Ⓖ Ⓗ Ⓙ	48 Ⓕ Ⓖ Ⓗ Ⓙ	56 Ⓕ Ⓖ Ⓗ Ⓙ	64 Ⓕ Ⓖ Ⓗ Ⓙ	
33 Ⓐ Ⓑ Ⓒ Ⓓ	41 Ⓐ Ⓑ Ⓒ Ⓓ	49 Ⓐ Ⓑ Ⓒ Ⓓ	57 Ⓐ Ⓑ Ⓒ Ⓓ	65 Ⓐ Ⓑ Ⓒ Ⓓ	

Geometry Modeled Instruction

1 Ⓐ Ⓑ Ⓒ Ⓓ	6 Ⓕ Ⓖ Ⓗ Ⓙ	11 Ⓐ Ⓑ Ⓒ Ⓓ	16 Ⓕ Ⓖ Ⓗ Ⓙ	21 Ⓐ Ⓑ Ⓒ Ⓓ
2 Ⓕ Ⓖ Ⓗ Ⓙ	7 Ⓐ Ⓑ Ⓒ Ⓓ	12 Ⓕ Ⓖ Ⓗ Ⓙ	17 Ⓐ Ⓑ Ⓒ Ⓓ	22 Ⓕ Ⓖ Ⓗ Ⓙ
3 Ⓐ Ⓑ Ⓒ Ⓓ	8 Ⓕ Ⓖ Ⓗ Ⓙ	13 Ⓐ Ⓑ Ⓒ Ⓓ	18 Ⓕ Ⓖ Ⓗ Ⓙ	23 Ⓐ Ⓑ Ⓒ Ⓓ
4 Ⓕ Ⓖ Ⓗ Ⓙ	9 Ⓐ Ⓑ Ⓒ Ⓓ	14 Ⓕ Ⓖ Ⓗ Ⓙ	19 Ⓐ Ⓑ Ⓒ Ⓓ	24 Ⓕ Ⓖ Ⓗ Ⓙ
5 Ⓐ Ⓑ Ⓒ Ⓓ	10 Ⓕ Ⓖ Ⓗ Ⓙ	15 Ⓐ Ⓑ Ⓒ Ⓓ	20 Ⓕ Ⓖ Ⓗ Ⓙ	25 Ⓐ Ⓑ Ⓒ Ⓓ

Geometry Independent Practice

26 Ⓕ Ⓖ Ⓗ Ⓙ	34 Ⓕ Ⓖ Ⓗ Ⓙ	42 Ⓕ Ⓖ Ⓗ Ⓙ	50 Ⓕ Ⓖ Ⓗ Ⓙ	58 Ⓕ Ⓖ Ⓗ Ⓙ	66 Ⓕ Ⓖ Ⓗ Ⓙ
27 Ⓐ Ⓑ Ⓒ Ⓓ	35 Ⓐ Ⓑ Ⓒ Ⓓ	43 Ⓐ Ⓑ Ⓒ Ⓓ	51 Ⓐ Ⓑ Ⓒ Ⓓ	59 Ⓐ Ⓑ Ⓒ Ⓓ	67 Ⓐ Ⓑ Ⓒ Ⓓ
28 Ⓕ Ⓖ Ⓗ Ⓙ	36 Ⓕ Ⓖ Ⓗ Ⓙ	44 Ⓕ Ⓖ Ⓗ Ⓙ	52 Ⓕ Ⓖ Ⓗ Ⓙ	60 Ⓕ Ⓖ Ⓗ Ⓙ	68 Ⓕ Ⓖ Ⓗ Ⓙ
29 Ⓐ Ⓑ Ⓒ Ⓓ	37 Ⓐ Ⓑ Ⓒ Ⓓ	45 Ⓐ Ⓑ Ⓒ Ⓓ	53 Ⓐ Ⓑ Ⓒ Ⓓ	61 Ⓐ Ⓑ Ⓒ Ⓓ	
30 Ⓕ Ⓖ Ⓗ Ⓙ	38 Ⓕ Ⓖ Ⓗ Ⓙ	46 Ⓕ Ⓖ Ⓗ Ⓙ	54 Ⓕ Ⓖ Ⓗ Ⓙ	62 Ⓕ Ⓖ Ⓗ Ⓙ	
31 Ⓐ Ⓑ Ⓒ Ⓓ	39 Ⓐ Ⓑ Ⓒ Ⓓ	47 Ⓐ Ⓑ Ⓒ Ⓓ	55 Ⓐ Ⓑ Ⓒ Ⓓ	63 Ⓐ Ⓑ Ⓒ Ⓓ	
32 Ⓕ Ⓖ Ⓗ Ⓙ	40 Ⓕ Ⓖ Ⓗ Ⓙ	48 Ⓕ Ⓖ Ⓗ Ⓙ	56 Ⓕ Ⓖ Ⓗ Ⓙ	64 Ⓕ Ⓖ Ⓗ Ⓙ	
33 Ⓐ Ⓑ Ⓒ Ⓓ	41 Ⓐ Ⓑ Ⓒ Ⓓ	49 Ⓐ Ⓑ Ⓒ Ⓓ	57 Ⓐ Ⓑ Ⓒ Ⓓ	65 Ⓐ Ⓑ Ⓒ Ⓓ	

Statistics and Probability Modeled Instruction

1 Ⓐ Ⓑ Ⓒ Ⓓ	6 Ⓕ Ⓖ Ⓗ Ⓙ	11 Ⓐ Ⓑ Ⓒ Ⓓ	16 Ⓕ Ⓖ Ⓗ Ⓙ	21 Ⓐ Ⓑ Ⓒ Ⓓ
2 Ⓕ Ⓖ Ⓗ Ⓙ	7 Ⓐ Ⓑ Ⓒ Ⓓ	12 Ⓕ Ⓖ Ⓗ Ⓙ	17 Ⓐ Ⓑ Ⓒ Ⓓ	22 Ⓕ Ⓖ Ⓗ Ⓙ
3 Ⓐ Ⓑ Ⓒ Ⓓ	8 Ⓕ Ⓖ Ⓗ Ⓙ	13 Ⓐ Ⓑ Ⓒ Ⓓ	18 Ⓕ Ⓖ Ⓗ Ⓙ	23 Ⓐ Ⓑ Ⓒ Ⓓ
4 Ⓕ Ⓖ Ⓗ Ⓙ	9 Ⓐ Ⓑ Ⓒ Ⓓ	14 Ⓕ Ⓖ Ⓗ Ⓙ	19 Ⓐ Ⓑ Ⓒ Ⓓ	24 Ⓕ Ⓖ Ⓗ Ⓙ
5 Ⓐ Ⓑ Ⓒ Ⓓ	10 Ⓕ Ⓖ Ⓗ Ⓙ	15 Ⓐ Ⓑ Ⓒ Ⓓ	20 Ⓕ Ⓖ Ⓗ Ⓙ	25 Ⓐ Ⓑ Ⓒ Ⓓ

Statistics and Probability Independent Practice

26 Ⓕ Ⓖ Ⓗ Ⓙ	31 Ⓐ Ⓑ Ⓒ Ⓓ	36 Ⓕ Ⓖ Ⓗ Ⓙ	41 Ⓐ Ⓑ Ⓒ Ⓓ	46 Ⓕ Ⓖ Ⓗ Ⓙ
27 Ⓐ Ⓑ Ⓒ Ⓓ	32 Ⓕ Ⓖ Ⓗ Ⓙ	37 Ⓐ Ⓑ Ⓒ Ⓓ	42 Ⓕ Ⓖ Ⓗ Ⓙ	47 Ⓐ Ⓑ Ⓒ Ⓓ
28 Ⓕ Ⓖ Ⓗ Ⓙ	33 Ⓐ Ⓑ Ⓒ Ⓓ	38 Ⓕ Ⓖ Ⓗ Ⓙ	43 Ⓐ Ⓑ Ⓒ Ⓓ	48 Ⓕ Ⓖ Ⓗ Ⓙ
20 Ⓐ Ⓑ Ⓒ Ⓓ	34 Ⓕ Ⓖ Ⓗ Ⓙ	39 Ⓐ Ⓑ Ⓒ Ⓓ	44 Ⓕ Ⓖ Ⓗ Ⓙ	49 Ⓐ Ⓑ Ⓒ Ⓓ
30 Ⓕ Ⓖ Ⓗ Ⓙ	35 Ⓐ Ⓑ Ⓒ Ⓓ	40 Ⓕ Ⓖ Ⓗ Ⓙ	45 Ⓐ Ⓑ Ⓒ Ⓓ	50 Ⓕ Ⓖ Ⓗ Ⓙ

Practice Test A

1 Ⓐ Ⓑ Ⓒ Ⓓ	10 Ⓕ Ⓖ Ⓗ Ⓙ	19 Ⓐ Ⓑ Ⓒ Ⓓ	28 Ⓕ Ⓖ Ⓗ Ⓙ	37 Ⓐ Ⓑ Ⓒ Ⓓ	46 Ⓕ Ⓖ Ⓗ Ⓙ
2 Ⓕ Ⓖ Ⓗ Ⓙ	11 Ⓐ Ⓑ Ⓒ Ⓓ	20 Ⓕ Ⓖ Ⓗ Ⓙ	29 Ⓐ Ⓑ Ⓒ Ⓓ	38 Ⓕ Ⓖ Ⓗ Ⓙ	47 Ⓐ Ⓑ Ⓒ Ⓓ
3 Ⓐ Ⓑ Ⓒ Ⓓ	12 Ⓕ Ⓖ Ⓗ Ⓙ	21 Ⓐ Ⓑ Ⓒ Ⓓ	30 Ⓕ Ⓖ Ⓗ Ⓙ	39 Ⓐ Ⓑ Ⓒ Ⓓ	48 Ⓕ Ⓖ Ⓗ Ⓙ
4 Ⓕ Ⓖ Ⓗ Ⓙ	13 Ⓐ Ⓑ Ⓒ Ⓓ	22 Ⓕ Ⓖ Ⓗ Ⓙ	31 Ⓐ Ⓑ Ⓒ Ⓓ	40 Ⓕ Ⓖ Ⓗ Ⓙ	49 Ⓐ Ⓑ Ⓒ Ⓓ
5 Ⓐ Ⓑ Ⓒ Ⓓ	14 Ⓕ Ⓖ Ⓗ Ⓙ	23 Ⓐ Ⓑ Ⓒ Ⓓ	32 Ⓕ Ⓖ Ⓗ Ⓙ	41 Ⓐ Ⓑ Ⓒ Ⓓ	50 Ⓕ Ⓖ Ⓗ Ⓙ
6 Ⓕ Ⓖ Ⓗ Ⓙ	15 Ⓐ Ⓑ Ⓒ Ⓓ	24 Ⓕ Ⓖ Ⓗ Ⓙ	33 Ⓐ Ⓑ Ⓒ Ⓓ	42 Ⓕ Ⓖ Ⓗ Ⓙ	
7 Ⓐ Ⓑ Ⓒ Ⓓ	16 Ⓕ Ⓖ Ⓗ Ⓙ	25 Ⓐ Ⓑ Ⓒ Ⓓ	34 Ⓕ Ⓖ Ⓗ Ⓙ	43 Ⓐ Ⓑ Ⓒ Ⓓ	
8 Ⓕ Ⓖ Ⓗ Ⓙ	17 Ⓐ Ⓑ Ⓒ Ⓓ	26 Ⓕ Ⓖ Ⓗ Ⓙ	35 Ⓐ Ⓑ Ⓒ Ⓓ	44 Ⓕ Ⓖ Ⓗ Ⓙ	
9 Ⓐ Ⓑ Ⓒ Ⓓ	18 Ⓕ Ⓖ Ⓗ Ⓙ	27 Ⓐ Ⓑ Ⓒ Ⓓ	36 Ⓕ Ⓖ Ⓗ Ⓙ	45 Ⓐ Ⓑ Ⓒ Ⓓ	

Practice Test B

1 Ⓐ Ⓑ Ⓒ Ⓓ	10 Ⓕ Ⓖ Ⓗ Ⓙ	19 Ⓐ Ⓑ Ⓒ Ⓓ	28 Ⓕ Ⓖ Ⓗ Ⓙ	37 Ⓐ Ⓑ Ⓒ Ⓓ	46 Ⓕ Ⓖ Ⓗ Ⓙ
2 Ⓕ Ⓖ Ⓗ Ⓙ	11 Ⓐ Ⓑ Ⓒ Ⓓ	20 Ⓕ Ⓖ Ⓗ Ⓙ	29 Ⓐ Ⓑ Ⓒ Ⓓ	38 Ⓕ Ⓖ Ⓗ Ⓙ	47 Ⓐ Ⓑ Ⓒ Ⓓ
3 Ⓐ Ⓑ Ⓒ Ⓓ	12 Ⓕ Ⓖ Ⓗ Ⓙ	21 Ⓐ Ⓑ Ⓒ Ⓓ	30 Ⓕ Ⓖ Ⓗ Ⓙ	39 Ⓐ Ⓑ Ⓒ Ⓓ	48 Ⓕ Ⓖ Ⓗ Ⓙ
4 Ⓕ Ⓖ Ⓗ Ⓙ	13 Ⓐ Ⓑ Ⓒ Ⓓ	22 Ⓕ Ⓖ Ⓗ Ⓙ	31 Ⓐ Ⓑ Ⓒ Ⓓ	40 Ⓕ Ⓖ Ⓗ Ⓙ	49 Ⓐ Ⓑ Ⓒ Ⓓ
5 Ⓐ Ⓑ Ⓒ Ⓓ	14 Ⓕ Ⓖ Ⓗ Ⓙ	23 Ⓐ Ⓑ Ⓒ Ⓓ	32 Ⓕ Ⓖ Ⓗ Ⓙ	41 Ⓐ Ⓑ Ⓒ Ⓓ	50 Ⓕ Ⓖ Ⓗ Ⓙ
6 Ⓕ Ⓖ Ⓗ Ⓙ	15 Ⓐ Ⓑ Ⓒ Ⓓ	24 Ⓕ Ⓖ Ⓗ Ⓙ	33 Ⓐ Ⓑ Ⓒ Ⓓ	42 Ⓕ Ⓖ Ⓗ Ⓙ	
7 Ⓐ Ⓑ Ⓒ Ⓓ	16 Ⓕ Ⓖ Ⓗ Ⓙ	25 Ⓐ Ⓑ Ⓒ Ⓓ	34 Ⓕ Ⓖ Ⓗ Ⓙ	43 Ⓐ Ⓑ Ⓒ Ⓓ	
8 Ⓕ Ⓖ Ⓗ Ⓙ	17 Ⓐ Ⓑ Ⓒ Ⓓ	26 Ⓕ Ⓖ Ⓗ Ⓙ	35 Ⓐ Ⓑ Ⓒ Ⓓ	44 Ⓕ Ⓖ Ⓗ Ⓙ	
9 Ⓐ Ⓑ Ⓒ Ⓓ	18 Ⓕ Ⓖ Ⓗ Ⓙ	27 Ⓐ Ⓑ Ⓒ Ⓓ	36 Ⓕ Ⓖ Ⓗ Ⓙ	45 Ⓐ Ⓑ Ⓒ Ⓓ	

Answer Key

Pretest

1. D [6.RP.1]
2. H [6.RP.2]
3. C [6.RP.3.a]
4. G [6.RP.3.b]
5. C [6.RP.3.c]
6. H [6.RP.3.d]
7. C [6.NS.1]
8. F [6.NS.2]
9. B [6.NS.3]
10. G [6.NS.4]
11. A [6.NS.5]
12. G [6.NS.6.a]
13. B [6.NS.6.b]
14. G [6.NS.6.c]
15. D [6.NS.7.a]
16. F [6.NS.7.b]
17. B [6.NS.7.c]
18. J [6.NS.7.d]
19. D [6.NS.8]
20. G [6.EE.1]
21. C [6.EE.2.a]
22. J [6.EE.2.b]
23. C [6.EE.2.c]
24. H [6.EE.3]
25. C [6.EE.4]
26. J [6.EE.5]
27. D [6.EE.6]
28. F [6.EE.7]
29. D [6.EE.8]
30. H [6.EE.9]
31. C [6.G.1]
32. H [6.G.1]
33. D [6.G.1]
34. H [6.G.1]
35. B [6.G.1]

36. F [6.G.2]
37. C [6.G.2]
38. F [6.G.3]
39. B [6.G.3]
40. F [6.G.4]
41. D [6.G.4]
42. F [6.SP.1]
43. C [6.SP.2]
44. G [6.SP.3]
45. D [6.SP.4]
46. H [6.SP.5.a]
47. B [6.SP.5.b]
48. H [6.SP.5.c]
49. C [6.SP.5.c]
50. J [6.SP.5.d]

Ratio and Proportion

Modeled Instruction

1. B [6.RP.1]
2. F [6.RP.1]
3. B [6.RP.1]
4. J [6.RP.1]
5. C [6.RP.2]
6. J [6.RP.2]
7. A [6.RP.2]
8. J [6.RP.2]
9. D [6.RP.3.a]
10. F [6.RP.3.a]
11. A [6.RP.3.a]
12. F [6.RP.3.a]
13. B [6.RP.3.a]
14. H [6.RP.3.b]
15. C [6.RP.3.b]
16. F [6.RP.3.b]
17. B [6.RP.3.b]
18. F [6.RP.3.c]

19. C [6.RP.3.c]
20. H [6.RP.3.c]
21. D [6.RP.3.c]
22. H [6.RP.3.d]
23. B [6.RP.3.d]
24. J [6.RP.3.d]
25. A [6.RP.3.d]

Ratio and Proportion
Independent Practice

26. G [6.RP.1]
27. D [6.RP.1]
28. J [6.RP.1]
29. A [6.RP.1]
30. F [6.RP.1]
31. B [6.RP.1]
32. H [6.RP.2]
33. C [6.RP.2]
34. F [6.RP.2]
35. B [6.RP.3.a]
36. G [6.RP.3.a]
37. A [6.RP.3.a]
38. G [6.RP.3.a]
39. D [6.RP.3.a]
40. H [6.RP.3.a]
41. A [6.RP.3.a]
42. G [6.RP.3.a]
43. A [6.RP.3.b]
44. H [6.RP.3.b]
45. C [6.RP.3.b]
46. J [6.RP.3.c]
47. B [6.RP.3.c]
48. G [6.RP.3.c]
49. A [6.RP.3.c]
50. H [6.RP.3.c]
51. D [6.RP.3.c]
52. G [6.RP.3.c]
53. A [6.RP.3.c]
54. J [6.RP.3.c]

55. C [6.RP.3.c]
56. J [6.RP.3.d]
57. C [6.RP.3.d]
58. F [6.RP.3.d]
59. C [6.RP.3.d]
60. G [6.RP.3.d]

Number Sense
Modeled Instruction

1. C [6.NS.1]
2. F [6.NS.1]
3. B [6.NS.2]
4. H [6.NS.2]
5. D [6.NS.3]
6. G [6.NS.3]
7. B [6.NS.3]
8. H [6.NS.3]
9. C [6.NS.4]
10. J [6.NS.4]
11. A [6.NS.4]
12. F [6.NS.5]
13. C [6.NS.6.a]
14. H [6.NS.6.a]
15. C [6.NS.6.b]
16. F [6.NS.6.b]
17. D [6.NS.6.c]
18. F [6.NS.6.c]
19. A [6.NS.6.c]
20. J [6.NS.6.c]
21. B [6.NS.7.a]
22. G [6.NS.7.b]
23. B [6.NS.7.c]
24. G [6.NS.7.d]
25. A [6.NS.8]

Number Sense

Independent Practice

26. H [6.NS.1]
27. C [6.NS.1]
28. H [6.NS.1]
29. B [6.NS.1]
30. J [6.NS.1]
31. B [6.NS.2]
32. F [6.NS.2]
33. C [6.NS.2]
34. G [6.NS.2]
35. B [6.NS.3]
36. H [6.NS.3]
37. D [6.NS.3]
38. G [6.NS.3]
39. C [6.NS.3]
40. F [6.NS.3]
41. B [6.NS.4]
42. G [6.NS.4]
43. B [6.NS.4]
44. H [6.NS.4]
45. D [6.NS.4]
46. G [6.NS.5]
47. C [6.NS.5]
48. F [6.NS.5]
49. A [6.NS.6.a]
50. J [6.NS.6.a]
51. B [6.NS.6.a]
52. G [6.NS.6.b]
53. D [6.NS.6.b]
54. H [6.NS.6.b]
55. B [6.NS.6.c]
56. J [6.NS.6.c]
57. A [6.NS.6.c]
58. G [6.NS.7.a]
59. B [6.NS.7.a]
60. J [6.NS.7.a]
61. D [6.NS.7.b]

62. J [6.NS.7.b]
63. D [6.NS.7.c]
64. G [6.NS.7.c]
65. A [6.NS.7.c]
66. F [6.NS.7.d]
67. A [6.NS.7.d]
68. F [6.NS.7.d]
69. C [6.NS.8]
70. J [6.NS.8]
71. C [6.NS.8]
72. G [6.NS.8]

Expressions and Equations

Modeled Instruction

1. A [6.EE.1]
2. J [6.EE.1]
3. A [6.EE.2.a]
4. G [6.EE.2.a]
5. C [6.EE.2.b]
6. J [6.EE.2.b]
7. A [6.EE.2.c]
8. G [6.EE.2.c]
9. D [6.EE.3]
10. F [6.EE.3]
11. D [6.EE.4]
12. G [6.EE.4]
13. A [6.EE.5]
14. J [6.EE.5]
15. A [6.EE.5]
16. H [6.EE.6]
17. C [6.EE.6]
18. G [6.EE.6]
19. D [6.EE.7]
20. H [6.EE.7]
21. A [6.EE.7]
22. H [6.EE.8]
23. B [6.EE.8]
24. H [6.EE.9]

25. A [6.EE.9]

Expressions and Equations
Independent Practice

26. H [6.EE.1]

27. B [6.EE.1]

28. G [6.EE.1]

29. D [6.EE.1]

30. H [6.EE.1]

31. B [6.EE.2.a]

32. J [6.EE.2.a]

33. A [6.EE.2.a]

34. F [6.EE.2.a]

35. B [6.EE.2.b]

36. F [6.EE.2.b]

37. D [6.EE.2.b]

38. G [6.EE.2.c]

39. B [6.EE.2.c]

40. J [6.EE.2.c]

41. A [6.EE.2.c]

42. H [6.EE.3]

43. C [6.EE.3]

44. G [6.EE.3]

45. D [6.EE.3]

46. J [6.EE.4]

47. D [6.EE.4]

48. J [6.EE.4]

49. D [6.EE.4]

50. H [6.EE.5]

51. C [6.EE.5]

52. F [6.EE.5]

53. C [6.EE.5]

54. H [6.EE.6]

55. D [6.EE.6]

56. H [6.EE.6]

57. A [6.EE.6]

58. J [6.EE.7]

59. C [6.EE.7]

60. F [6.EE.7]

61. B [6.EE.7]

62. G [6.EE.8]

63. D [6.EE.8]

64. F [6.EE.8]

65. D [6.EE.8]

66. G [6.EE.9]

67. D [6.EE.9]

68. H [6.EE.9]

69. A [6.EE.9]

70. G [6.EE.9]

Geometry
Modeled Instruction

1. D [6.G.1]

2. H [6.G.1]

3. C [6.G.1]

4. H [6.G.1]

5. D [6.G.1]

6. G [6.G.1]

7. B [6.G.1]

8. H [6.G.1]

9. A [6.G.2]

10. H [6.G.2]

11. D [6.G.2]

12. H [6.G.2]

13. C [6.G.3]

14. H [6.G.3]

15. B [6.G.3]

16. H [6.G.3]

17. A [6.G.3]

18. G [6.G.3]

19. D [6.G.4]

20. F [6.G.4]

21. D [6.G.4]

22. F [6.G.4]

23. D [6.G.4]
24. H [6.G.4]
25. A [6.G.4]

Geometry
Independent Practice
26. J [6.G.1]
27. B [6.G.1]
28. H [6.G.1]
29. D [6.G.1]
30. F [6.G.1]
31. A [6.G.1]
32. G [6.G.1]
33. B [6.G.1]
34. H [6.G.1]
35. C [6.G.1]
36. G [6.G.1]
37. A [6.G.1]
38. J [6.G.1]
39. C [6.G.1]
40. F [6.G.1]
41. D [6.G.2]
42. F [6.G.2]
43. B [6.G.2]
44. H [6.G.2]
45. C [6.G.2]
46. J [6.G.2]
47. B [6.G.2]
48. H [6.G.2]
49. C [6.G.3]
50. H [6.G.3]
51. D [6.G.3]
52. H [6.G.3]
53. C [6.G.3]
54. G [6.G.3]
55. B [6.G.3]
56. J [6.G.3]

57. B [6.G.3]
58. F [6.G.3]
59. C [6.G.3]
60. H [6.G.4]
61. A [6.G.4]
62. H [6.G.4]
63. B [6.G.4]
64. G [6.G.4]
65. A [6.G.4]
66. G [6.G.4]
67. B [6.G.4]
68. H [6.G.4]

Statistics and Probability
Modeled Instruction
1. D [6.SP.1]
2. H [6.SP.1]
3. A [6.SP.1]
4. H [6.SP.2]
5. B [6.SP.2]
6. H [6.SP.2]
7. D [6.SP.3]
8. H [6.SP.3]
9. A [6.SP.3]
10. G [6.SP.4]
11. C [6.SP.4]
12. J [6.SP.4]
13. A [6.SP.5.a]
14. J [6.SP.5.a]
15. B [6.SP.5.a]
16. J [6.SP.5.b]
17. D [6.SP.5.c]
18. G [6.SP.5.c]
19. B [6.SP.5.c]
20. J [6.SP.5.c]
21. A [6.SP.5.c]
22. H [6.SP.5.c]

23. D [6.SP.5.d]

24. H [6.SP.5.d]

25. A [6.SP.5.d]

Statistics and Probability

Independent Practice

26. F [6.SP.1]

27. D [6.SP.1]

28. H [6.SP.1]

29. A [6.SP.1]

30. J [6.SP.2]

31. B [6.SP.2]

32. G [6.SP.2]

33. B [6.SP.2]

34. H [6.SP.3]

35. A [6.SP.3]

36. F [6.SP.4]

37. C [6.SP.4]

38. J [6.SP.4]

39. C [6.SP.4]

40. G [6.SP.5.a]

41. C [6.SP.5.a]

42. J [6.SP.5.a]

43. A [6.SP.5.b]

44. G [6.SP.5.b]

45. B [6.SP.5.b]

46. G [6.SP.5.c]

47. D [6.SP.5.c]

48. H [6.SP.5.c]

49. D [6.SP.5.d]

50. F [6.SP.5.d]

Practice Test A

1. D [6.EE.3]

2. G [6.RP.1]

3. A [6.NS.7.a]

4. J [6.G.1]

5. D [6.SP.1]

6. J [6.SP.5.d]

7. B [6.EE.2.c]

8. G [6.NS.6.c]

9. B [6.RP.3.a]

10. F [6.NS.1]

11. C [6.EE.4]

12. G [6.NS.6.a]

13. A [6.RP.2]

14. G [6.EE.8]

15. C [6.G.2]

16. F [6.SP.2]

17. B [6.G.4]

18. G [6.EE.9]

19. C [6.EE.2.a]

20. G [6.RP.3.d]

21. D [6.EE.5]

22. H [6.RP.3.b]

23. B [6.NS.2]

24. H [6.EE.1]

25. C [6.SP.3]

26. H [6.G.3]

27. C [6.EE.6]

28. H [6.NS.7.d]

29. B [6.RP.3.c]

30. J [6.NS.3]

31. B [6.EE.7]

32. G [6.NS.6.b]

33. A [6.EE.2.b]

34. J [6.G.4]

35. B [6.SP.4]

36. G [6.NS.7.b]

37. A [6.NS.5]

38. G [6.SP.5.a]

39. A [6.NS.8]

40. J [6.G.3]

41. B [6.NS.7.c]

42. J [6.SP.5.b]

43. D [6.NS.4]

44. H [6.SP.5.c]

45. A [6.G.3]

Answer Key

Higher Scores on Math, Grade 6

46. F [6.NS.2]
47. B [6.EE.1]
48. H [6.RP.3.b]
49. C [6.G.1]
50. G [6.SP.5.b]

Practice Test B

1. D [6.SP.5.a]
2. H [6.RP.1]
3. C [6.NS.3]
4. G [6.EE.6]
5. B [6.G.1]
6. F [6.SP.2]
7. D [6.EE.5]
8. H [6.NS.1]
9. B [6.RP.2]
10. H [6.EE.7]
11. C [6.NS.7.a]
12. F [6.G.2]
13. B [6.SP.1]
14. G [6.EE.9]
15. C [6.G.3]
16. J [6.SP.3]
17. A [6.EE.2.a]
18. G [6.NS.8]
19. D [6.RP.3.a]
20. G [6.NS.2]
21. A [6.EE.1]
22. G [6.RP.3.b]
23. C [6.NS.4]
24. F [6.EE.3]
25. D [6.G.4]
26. G [6.SP.5.b]
27. C [6.EE.8]
28. J [6.NS.7.b]
29. B [6.SP.4]
30. G [6.NS.6.a]
31. C [6.EE.4]
32. H [6.NS.5]

33. D [6.RP.3.c]
34. F [6.SP.5.c]
35. A [6.G.2]
36. J [6.EE.2.b]
37. A [6.NS.6.b]
38. J [6.RP.3.d]
39. A [6.EE.2.c]
40. H [6.NS.6.c]
41. C [6.SP.5.d]
42. J [6.NS.7.c]
43. B [6.RP.2]
44. H [6.NS.7.d]
45. B [6.EE.3]
46. G [6.G.1]
47. A [6.SP.2]
48. G [6.NS.3]
49. D [6.G.4]
50. F [6.EE.6]

rence Sheet

Length

Customary

1 mile (mi) = 5,280 feet (ft)

1 mile (mi) = 1,760 yards (yd)

1 yard (yd) = 3 feet (ft)

1 foot (ft) = 12 inches (in.)

Metric

1 kilometer (km) = 1,000 meters (m)

1 meter (m) = 100 centimeters (cm)

1 centimeter (cm) = 10 millimeters (mm)

Volume and Capacity

Customary

1 gallon (gal) = 128 fluid ounces (fl oz)

1 gallon (gal) = 4 quarts (qt)

1 quart (qt) = 2 pints (pt)

1 pint (pt) = 2 cups (c)

1 cup (c) = 8 fluid ounces (fl oz)

Metric

1 liter (L) = 1,000 milliliters (mL)

Weight and Mass

Customary

1 ton (T) = 2,000 pounds (lb)

1 pound (lb) = 16 ounces (oz)

Metric

1 kilogram (kg) = 1,000 grams (g)

1 gram (g) = 1,000 milligrams (mg)

Perimeter

Square	$P = 4s$
Rectangle	$P = 2l + 2w$ or $P = 2\,(l + w)$

Circumference

Circle	$C = 2\pi r$ or $C = \pi d$

Area

Square	$A = s \times s$ or $A = s^2$
Rectangle	$A = l \times w$
Triangle	$A = \frac{1}{2}\,bh$ or $A = \frac{bh}{2}$
Trapezoid	$A = \frac{1}{2}\,(b_1 + b_2)h$ or $A = \frac{(b_1 + b_2)h}{2}$
Circle	$A = \pi r^2$
Parallelogram	$A = bh$

Volume

Cube	$V = s \times s \times s$ or $V = s^3$
Rectangular Prism	$V = lwh$

Pi

π	$\pi \approx 3.14$ or $\pi \approx \frac{22}{7}$

Time

1 year = 365 days

1 year = 12 months

1 year = 52 weeks

1 week = 7 days

1 day = 24 hours

1 hour = 60 minutes

1 minute = 60 seconds

Reference Sheet
Higher Scores on Math, Grade 6

23. D [6.G.4]

24. H [6.G.4]

25. A [6.G.4]

Geometry

Independent Practice

26. J [6.G.1]

27. B [6.G.1]

28. H [6.G.1]

29. D [6.G.1]

30. F [6.G.1]

31. A [6.G.1]

32. G [6.G.1]

33. B [6.G.1]

34. H [6.G.1]

35. C [6.G.1]

36. G [6.G.1]

37. A [6.G.1]

38. J [6.G.1]

39. C [6.G.1]

40. F [6.G.1]

41. D [6.G.2]

42. F [6.G.2]

43. B [6.G.2]

44. H [6.G.2]

45. C [6.G.2]

46. J [6.G.2]

47. B [6.G.2]

48. H [6.G.2]

49. C [6.G.3]

50. H [6.G.3]

51. D [6.G.3]

52. H [6.G.3]

53. C [6.G.3]

54. G [6.G.3]

55. B [6.G.3]

56. J [6.G.3]

57. B [6.G.3]

58. F [6.G.3]

59. C [6.G.3]

60. H [6.G.4]

61. A [6.G.4]

62. H [6.G.4]

63. B [6.G.4]

64. G [6.G.4]

65. A [6.G.4]

66. G [6.G.4]

67. B [6.G.4]

68. H [6.G.4]

Statistics and Probability

Modeled Instruction

1. D [6.SP.1]

2. H [6.SP.1]

3. A [6.SP.1]

4. H [6.SP.2]

5. B [6.SP.2]

6. H [6.SP.2]

7. D [6.SP.3]

8. H [6.SP.3]

9. A [6.SP.3]

10. G [6.SP.4]

11. C [6.SP.4]

12. J [6.SP.4]

13. A [6.SP.5.a]

14. J [6.SP.5.a]

15. B [6.SP.5.a]

16. J [6.SP.5.b]

17. D [6.SP.5.c]

18. G [6.SP.5.c]

19. B [6.SP.5.c]

20. J [6.SP.5.c]

21. A [6.SP.5.c]

22. H [6.SP.5.c]

23. D [6.SP.5.d]

24. H [6.SP.5.d]

25. A [6.SP.5.d]

Statistics and Probability

Independent Practice

26. F [6.SP.1]

27. D [6.SP.1]

28. H [6.SP.1]

29. A [6.SP.1]

30. J [6.SP.2]

31. B [6.SP.2]

32. G [6.SP.2]

33. B [6.SP.2]

34. H [6.SP.3]

35. A [6.SP.3]

36. F [6.SP.4]

37. C [6.SP.4]

38. J [6.SP.4]

39. C [6.SP.4]

40. G [6.SP.5.a]

41. C [6.SP.5.a]

42. J [6.SP.5.a]

43. A [6.SP.5.b]

44. G [6.SP.5.b]

45. B [6.SP.5.b]

46. G [6.SP.5.c]

47. D [6.SP.5.c]

48. H [6.SP.5.c]

49. D [6.SP.5.d]

50. F [6.SP.5.d]

Practice Test A

1. D [6.EE.3]

2. G [6.RP.1]

3. A [6.NS.7.a]

4. J [6.G.1]

5. D [6.SP.1]

6. J [6.SP.5.d]

7. B [6.EE.2.c]

8. G [6.NS.6.c]

9. B [6.RP.3.a]

10. F [6.NS.1]

11. C [6.EE.4]

12. G [6.NS.6.a]

13. A [6.RP.2]

14. G [6.EE.8]

15. C [6.G.2]

16. F [6.SP.2]

17. B [6.G.4]

18. G [6.EE.9]

19. C [6.EE.2.a]

20. G [6.RP.3.d]

21. D [6.EE.5]

22. H [6.RP.3.b]

23. B [6.NS.2]

24. H [6.EE.1]

25. C [6.SP.3]

26. H [6.G.3]

27. C [6.EE.6]

28. H [6.NS.7.d]

29. B [6.RP.3.c]

30. J [6.NS.3]

31. B [6.EE.7]

32. G [6.NS.6.b]

33. A [6.EE.2.b]

34. J [6.G.4]

35. B [6.SP.4]

36. G [6.NS.7.b]

37. A [6.NS.5]

38. G [6.SP.5.a]

39. A [6.NS.8]

40. J [6.G.3]

41. B [6.NS.7.c]

42. J [6.SP.5.b]

43. D [6.NS.4]

44. H [6.SP.5.c]

45. A [6.G.3]

46. F [6.NS.2]
47. B [6.EE.1]
48. H [6.RP.3.b]
49. C [6.G.1]
50. G [6.SP.5.b]

Practice Test B

1. D [6.SP.5.a]
2. H [6.RP.1]
3. C [6.NS.3]
4. G [6.EE.6]
5. B [6.G.1]
6. F [6.SP.2]
7. D [6.EE.5]
8. H [6.NS.1]
9. B [6.RP.2]
10. H [6.EE.7]
11. C [6.NS.7.a]
12. F [6.G.2]
13. B [6.SP.1]
14. G [6.EE.9]
15. C [6.G.3]
16. J [6.SP.3]
17. A [6.EE.2.a]
18. G [6.NS.8]
19. D [6.RP.3.a]
20. G [6.NS.2]
21. A [6.EE.1]
22. G [6.RP.3.b]
23. C [6.NS.4]
24. F [6.EE.3]
25. D [6.G.4]
26. G [6.SP.5.b]
27. C [6.EE.8]
28. J [6.NS.7.b]
29. B [6.SP.4]
30. G [6.NS.6.a]
31. C [6.EE.4]
32. H [6.NS.5]

33. D [6.RP.3.c]
34. F [6.SP.5.c]
35. A [6.G.2]
36. J [6.EE.2.b]
37. A [6.NS.6.b]
38. J [6.RP.3.d]
39. A [6.EE.2.c]
40. H [6.NS.6.c]
41. C [6.SP.5.d]
42. J [6.NS.7.c]
43. B [6.RP.2]
44. H [6.NS.7.d]
45. B [6.EE.3]
46. G [6.G.1]
47. A [6.SP.2]
48. G [6.NS.3]
49. D [6.G.4]
50. F [6.EE.6]

Reference Sheet

Length

Customary

1 mile (mi) = 5,280 feet (ft)

1 mile (mi) = 1,760 yards (yd)

1 yard (yd) = 3 feet (ft)

1 foot (ft) = 12 inches (in.)

Metric

1 kilometer (km) = 1,000 meters (m)

1 meter (m) = 100 centimeters (cm)

1 centimeter (cm) = 10 millimeters (mm)

Volume and Capacity

Customary

1 gallon (gal) = 128 fluid ounces (fl oz)

1 gallon (gal) = 4 quarts (qt)

1 quart (qt) = 2 pints (pt)

1 pint (pt) = 2 cups (c)

1 cup (c) = 8 fluid ounces (fl oz)

Metric

1 liter (L) = 1,000 milliliters (mL)

Weight and Mass

Customary

1 ton (T) = 2,000 pounds (lb)

1 pound (lb) = 16 ounces (oz)

Metric

1 kilogram (kg) = 1,000 grams (g)

1 gram (g) = 1,000 milligrams (mg)

Perimeter

Square	$P = 4s$
Rectangle	$P = 2l + 2w$ or $P = 2(l + w)$

Circumference

Circle	$C = 2\pi r$ or $C = \pi d$

Area

Square	$A = s \times s$ or $A = s^2$
Rectangle	$A = l \times w$
Triangle	$A = \frac{1}{2} bh$ or $A = \frac{bh}{2}$
Trapezoid	$A = \frac{1}{2}(b_1 + b_2)h$ or $A = \frac{(b_1 + b_2)h}{2}$
Circle	$A = \pi r^2$
Parallelogram	$A = bh$

Volume

Cube	$V = s \times s \times s$ or $V = s^3$
Rectangular Prism	$V = lwh$

Pi

π	$\pi \approx 3.14$ or $\pi \approx \frac{22}{7}$

Time

1 year = 365 days

1 year = 12 months

1 year = 52 weeks

1 week = 7 days

1 day = 24 hours

1 hour = 60 minutes

1 minute = 60 seconds